THE MODERN NATIONS IN
HISTORICAL PERSPECTIVE

ROBIN W. WINKS, *General Editor*

The volumes in this series deal with individual nations or groups of closely related nations throughout the world, summarizing the chief historical trends and influences that have contributed to each nation's present-day character, problems, and behavior. Recent data are incorporated with established historical background to achieve a fresh synthesis and original interpretation.

JOHN EDWIN FAGG, the author of this volume, is Professor of History at New York University, Chairman of the Department of History in Washington Square College of that university, and director of its Portuguese-Brazilian Center. He has written *Latin America: A General History* (1963), *The Republican Movement in Spain* (1944), and articles on such figures as Isabel II of Spain, Rafael Altamira y Crevea, and Sir Charles Webster, as well as the introduction to *The Letters of Christopher Columbus*. He was a major contributor to the seven-volume official history, *The Army Air Forces in World War II* (1948-58).

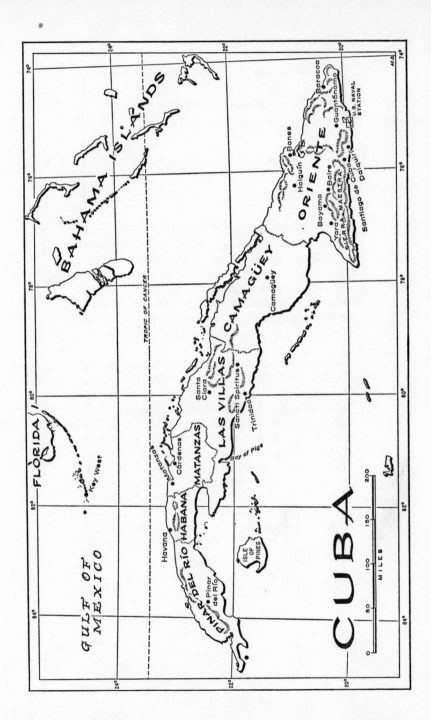

CUBA, HAITI,
& THE DOMINICAN REPUBLIC

JOHN EDWIN FAGG

A SPECTRUM BOOK

Prentice-Hall, Inc.

Englewood Cliffs, New Jersey

Current printing (last digit):

11 10 9 8 7 6 5 4 3

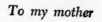

To my mother

Contents

CUBA, HAITI,
& THE DOMINICAN REPUBLIC

Three Neighbors with Divergent Careers

Cuba's situation and prospects today, matters of great importance to a watchful world, necessarily relate to those of its neighbors, Haiti and the Dominican Republic, on the island of Hispaniola. The geographical proximity of these two largest islands of the Caribbean and the many common historical experiences they share have not, however, caused the inhabitants of the three countries to feel strong bonds of sympathy or identification with one another. It is true that among the most humble classes there is a certain amount of movement from one land to the other as economic hardship or opportunity dictates, but Haitians and Dominicans are traditionally hostile to one another, and Cubans are scarcely friends with either. Among the rulers there continues to be, as there has always been, a tendency to meddle in the politics of the others, usually in a surreptitious fashion.

The three republics resemble one another in geography and climate; substantial portions of each are highly fertile, the scenery is beautiful, and the living is, or ought to be, good. All have long been dependent, for prosperity beyond mere subsistence, on more advanced foreign lands to purchase their products and to effect technological improvements. The three have reason to nurture resentment of these same outsiders, the favorite target being the United States, which has generally had uneasy and unstable relations with these islands and has done them immense good at times and some harm at others. American economic influence on the Dominican Republic has been important to that nation but, in all, rather modest. For most of its history Haiti has experienced little impact of American economic power. In

1

the case of Cuba, the United States acquired a dominant position in economic matters during World War I but began to subside after 1929 and lost out altogether under Fidel Castro.

The common history of the two islands includes their occupation by aborigines mainly of the Arawak language group, who probably migrated from South America through the Lesser Antilles. Cuba may have had a native population of 100,000. The earliest surviving human groups in 1492 were the Guanajatebeys, an Old Stone Age people who lived a nomadic existence in the western tip of the island. A New Stone Age group, the Ciboneys, inhabited the central part; the Tainos of the east, Arawakan like the Ciboneys, were still more advanced. The Tainos also occupied all of the island of Hispaniola, which was probably much more populous than Cuba. They used flint, made pottery, ornaments, and baskets, and engaged in primitive agriculture. Political organization centered about the clan, altogether so in Cuba but with clans grouped in five major monarchies in Hispaniola. These natives lived in a state of peace seldom found anywhere. Apparently they rarely warred with one another, and animal life was such that few beasts brought out their hunting skills or aggressive instincts. Except for the nomads of western Cuba, the aborigines usually dwelt in semipermanent villages composed of round houses of bamboo and palm thatch. They had canoes, some large enough for ocean sailing, and that remarkable invention that delighted the Europeans, the hammock. They ate fish, turtles, iguanas, snakes, and birds, as well as corn, sweet potatoes, chili, squash, peppers, nuts, and the invaluable plant known as cassava or manioc. Tobacco in the form of cigars and snuff was in very wide use. Although they made cotton cloth, the natives often preferred to be naked except for feathers, and they shocked the Spaniards by painting their bodies. Agreeable as these "Indians," as Columbus called them, first seemed to the Spaniards, they soon aroused disgust. In Spanish eyes these pagans of a semitropical paradise were soon transformed from noble savages into a repellent, unreliable race of inferiors who worshiped idols and engaged in mating practices that seemed to defy decency and nature.

The tragedy that befell the Indians was one of the most terrible developments in the history of the Caribbean region. European diseases account for the virtual extinction of the natives, though massacres and other brutalities on the part of the conquistadors were major contributing factors. And food shortages resulting from the disorganization of the primitive economy, overwork, worry, grief, suicide, infanticide, and flight were also instrumental. Within two generations after Columbus' first visit to the islands, scarcely any Indians were left. Humanitarian efforts by Father Bartolomé de Las Casas, successive Spanish monarchs, and occasional officials or clergymen could not arrest the depopulation. Even the Spanish occupiers underwent dreadful suffering and disappointment. Wood and a few exotic articles were poor rewards for the riches of the fabled Indies they had hoped to find. Gold dust, however, was abundant enough to maintain official interest in holding and developing the islands, that and rumors of splendid kingdoms beyond. Yet by 1511, when Santo Domingo had scarcely become a sound base for food and livestock production, its more energetic Spaniards migrated to areas of greater promise, among them Cuba. Viable as Cuba seemed as a colony by 1519, its most vigorous elements soon departed for Mexico, Panama, or Peru and later, with Hernando de Soto, for a disastrous incursion into the present-day United States. By the mid-sixteenth century, Hispaniola and Cuba had served their purpose as stepping-stones for Spanish expansion to the continent and remained as melancholy sacrifices to the Europeanization of the New World.

In the two centuries that followed, both islands languished. The Spanish element was small, backward, and often unruly. The Indians had all but vanished. Negro slaves were imported slowly, gradually redressing the ghastly population loss of the early colonial period. Santo Domingo, Santiago de Cuba, and a few other towns survived as dim sparks of Western civilization. Havana was more important, its protected harbor and location beside the Gulf Stream making it a center of Spanish naval defense for the Americas and a base for preparing the great treasure fleets for their voyages to Spain. In all, the islands were underpopulated and poorly developed. They produced little but food, livestock, and wood. Foreign enemies and various types of adventurers, criminals, and pirates operated in and out of them with increasing boldness during the seventeenth century. Some of these interlopers wrenched western Hispaniola, or Haiti, entirely away from Spain and it eventually fell under French power. In 1697 Spain formally recognized France's title to this land, which went its own way and never reentered the Spanish community. Jamaica and most of the Lesser Antilles had already been removed from Spanish control by that time.

During the eighteenth century Haiti, then Saint-Domingue, burgeoned dramatically into the most profitable European colony in the world, thanks to sugar production and the African slavery that supported it. Cuba and Santo Domingo gradually felt the effects of the Spanish regeneration under the Bourbon dynasty during that century, particularly after the end of the Seven Years' War. Cultivation of tobacco, coffee, and sugar, together with hides and timber, gave them some economic value, though they were eclipsed by the great mineral-producing Spanish viceroyalties on the mainland. Although a majority of the population was nonwhite, both colonies were definitely European-oriented. Tension between the Spanish-born peninsulars and the American-born whites, or creoles, sharpened during the revolutionary period of the late eighteenth and early nineteenth centuries. In French Saint-Domingue, a massive slave uprising virtually eliminated the whites and resulted in the independence of Haiti by 1804. When the creoles of Santo Domingo seceded from Spain in 1821, they promptly found their country absorbed by Haitians, who held it until 1844. Cuba and Puerto Rico remained in the Spanish monarchy until 1898.

Varying political careers of the three countries made for different economic and cultural and even racial evolution. Haiti became Negroid with a French orientation, defiant of the outside world, isolated, and a country of small farmers and little commerce or industry. The Dominican Republic became a largely mulatto land, obsessed with fear of Haiti. Until very recent times it too was a backward country of small farmers or ranchers. Cuba's economic development was far more complicated and significant. It long retained a pro-Spanish aristocracy as well as strong business and cultural ties with the outside world. With Negroes, mulattoes, and whites in almost equal proportion by the end of the colonial period, it remained nonetheless a Western country.

Spain's Imprint

For more than three centuries in the case of Santo Domingo and nearly four in the case of Cuba, the Spanish imperial or colonial system was the major historical influence. It scarcely affected Haiti at all. The overseas possessions in America, or the "Indies," were the property of the monarch of Castile from the time of Isabel the Catholic. Juridically, they were equal to the European domains of those sovereigns, but in fact, Castilians or other Spaniards held nearly all of the offices. Such persons were sent to the New World by the crown, and they served such brief terms and were rotated so frequently that they had little opportunity to identify themselves with the lands they ruled. During reigns in which the monarchs were incapable or indifferent, the American empire was managed by the Council of Indies, except for a period during the eighteenth century when a Ministry of Indies was ascendant. These bodies chose and directed the officials of the vast overseas commonwealth, regulated economic and commercial affairs, supervised the ecclesiastical establishment, and issued decrees that had the force of legislation on a wide variety of matters. Governors or captain-generals represented the executive power in Cuba and Santo Domingo, and lesser appointed officers extended the crown's authority, at least in theory, to the lowest levels. Few colonists cared or dared to challenge the system, which was designed to inspire obedience rather than respond to popular desires.

Ancillary agencies of royal power did little to inculcate habits of self-government. Majestic courts known as *audiencias* administered justice and occasionally asserted something resembling the doctrine of separation of powers, but never successfully for any length of time. The Church was in many ways an arm of the crown, its prelates nominated by Madrid and its finances and activities always under royal management. Rarely was the union of altar and throne strained. The garrisons and fleets based principally in Havana were under the monarch's orders; even the creation of colonial militias in the eighteenth century did not threaten the power of Spain in the islands, though it did in the mainland colonies. Town councils, or *cabildos*, represented the more important whites in local affairs. Yet even these bodies seldom resisted the weight of royal authority or weakened the executive tradition that has persisted so powerfully in Latin America.

To acknowledge the strength and long endurance of the Spanish colonial system is not to deny that the inhabitants often flouted the royal will. The island colonials avidly dealt with smugglers, outlaws, and foreign enemies when they had the chance. They disregarded many laws regarding humane treatment of Indians or Negroes, and they generally evaded taxation and undermined the commercial monopolies. Many, perhaps most, royal officials were themselves corrupt and eager to connive with subjects and foreigners in cheating the crown. The sheer underpopulation and isolation of the islands made all institutions frail, all efforts to flaunt the might and majesty of the royal government open to mockery. Cubans, especially, developed a tradition, which is far from moribund today, of circumventing the most stringent commands of rulers while professing to obey them.

The impress of Spain on Cuba and the Dominican Republic has been indelible in language, religion, and culture. Much as the Castilian language has been softened and blurred by Caribbean pronunciation or modified by local terms, it has steadily prevailed. Roman Catholicism has suffered in the Dominican Republic because of the long Haitian occupation, but it survived and regained most of the lost ground. Spanish anticlericalism and Cuban mellowness helped weaken it during the nineteenth century in the larger island, and the Cuban republic separated Church and state. Yet until recent years, it has been overwhelmingly the faith of Cuban believers. Many habits, attitudes, sports, games, and tastes of Spain have, of course, persisted, and in the case of Cuba have perhaps been strengthened because of the large peninsular immigration after independence. In view of its deliberate self-isolation, Haiti greatly weakened its ties with Roman Catholicism and French culture, though the small mulatto *élite* has been fairly successful in maintaining a connection with Rome and Paris.

Visible reminders of the Spanish colonial past remain in the numerous buildings—official palaces, churches, convents, fortifications, theaters, and residences—of towns in Cuba and the Dominican Republic, reflecting the changing tastes and techniques of architecture over the centuries, from the time when Columbus' son built a governor's palace in Santo Domingo until the 1890s. The pattern of towns and plantation construction attests to the cult of beauty and the passion for uniformity that Spain enforced.

In literature, extremely little was produced in the Caribbean colonies until Cuba grew to maturity in the nineteenth century. The cultured classes in that island often took pride in their Spanishness and shared almost as fully as peninsulars in the successive movements of Romanticism, Realism, Naturalism, and Modernism. Romanticism, which struck the Spanish world suddenly with the return of political exiles in the 1830s, offered Cubans a way to dramatize creole resentment against peninsulars, to praise liberty and extol the idea of independence, and to express compassion for slaves and other depressed groups. The poets Diego Gabriel de la Concepción Valdés ("Plácido"), José Jacinto Milanés, and Gertrudis Gómez de Avellaneda were probably the best of the mid-nineteenth century. Ricardo de Palma, Cirilo Villaverde, and José Antonio Echeverría were at least locally renowned as Romantic novelists. Only one Romantic Dominican stands out, a writer associated with the Spanish reoccupation of his country in the 1860s, Manuel de Jesús Galván, who described with sympathy both Spaniard and Indian in the early days of colonialism.

In the late colonial period philosophic writers and educators influenced the more responsible elements of Cuban opinion to think of public affairs, including Cuba's relations with Spain. Of these, Father Félix Varela was the earliest and most admired by university students. José Antonio Saco succeeded him as the idol of well-to-do youths and was exiled, though he was a loyal subject and continued for many years to preach that Cuba should work for a respectable status within the monarchy. José de la Luz y Caballero, who was once suspected of subversion, won an exalted place in the opinions of serious-minded Cubans who favored modernity and reform. Toward the end of the colonial period and into the twentieth century, Manuel Sanguily and Enrique José Varona continued a tradition that learned men should guide their compatriots in their thinking on national affairs as well as philosophy. A press that was often surprisingly high-minded was also a heritage of the colonial period.

Cuba's favorite hero, José Martí, labored to end colonialism. This extraordinarily talented creole defies epitomization, so torrential were his writings and so vast his literary gifts. Poet, novelist, thinker, journalist, orator, agitator, and "Apostle" of independence, he appealed to the noblest in Cuban character with a skill that gave new dimensions to Spanish as a language. His contemporary, the sickly and sad Julián del Casal, was the first and probably the greatest of Modernist poets in the island. Obsession with style among Hispano-Cuban poets continued to be pronounced until a decade after independence.

Freedom from Spain after 1898 did not cut Cuba loose from peninsular influences in literature. The failure of the island to flourish as an independent republic, however, probably increased the pessimistic strain that suffuses the Realistic and Naturalistic novels of the twentieth century and gives them a distinctive Cuban character. Far more than in the utterances of politicians, one sees uneasiness with respect to social injustices in the works of Jesús Castellanos, José Antonio Ramos, and Carlos Loveira and in the poems of vanguardists like Mariano Brull and Nicolás Guillén. As in Spain, whose literary rhythms Cuba followed, experimental poetry and novels of protest characterized the decade after World War I. By then the American cinema and manifold European influences also made themselves felt. Except for nostalgic conservatives, Cuban thought and literature turned away from Spain as the century went on, particularly after the victory of the Franco government in 1939. Alienation from traditional Christian values, as in Existentialism, and a despairing of democratic republicanism as well as anti-American attitudes characterized the writings of the mid-twentieth century. A very large proportion of men of letters accepted the basic assumptions of Marxism-Leninism some years before Fidel Castro, whose advent in 1959 signified a determined campaign to turn Cuban thought and expression against both Spain and the United States.

THE REVOLUTION IN PERSPECTIVE

Cuba's revolution has excited profound interest as a massive effort to transform one of the most strategically located lands in the New World. Genuine sympathy greeted the advent of Fidel Castro in 1959 in most quarters because it seemed to signify a dramatic break with the past and the opening of new channels to a better future. Cuban aspirations for democracy, social justice, and mastery of their own destiny held large implications for the rest of Latin America.

To be sure, few outsiders knew much about the the island at the time Castro came into power. It was easy for most people to accept the notion that this was a country of landlords and peasants, the former rich and beholden to foreign interests and the latter pitifully degraded. Since Cuba had long served as a veritable sugar bowl to the United States, and since American business had been deeply involved in its economy, its ills could plausibly be attributed to the smothering influence of the giant neighbor to the north. Moreover, the United States had directly intervened in Cuba on several occasions between 1898 and 1933 and had exercised an overpowering influence on its internal and foreign affairs afterward. Both officialdom and the public in the United States suffered from a sense of guilt for the pressures that had been brought on this little country, and much world opinion, with more fervor than fact, pointed to the United States as the true cause of conditions so intolerable that a revolution finally came about.

Enthusiasm for the Castro regime markedly declined in the following six years. The leader himself alienated many Cubans and foreigners who had initially regarded him as a hero. His words and actions revealed him as unstable, violent, tyrannical, and ready to provoke danger of the most extreme sort for the peace of the world. The floods of refugees bespoke much more than the scampering of rascals of the fallen regime to escape deserved retribution. Among them were many of Cuba's finest citizens. The sacrifices and risks they endured to emigrate, and the tales they told, emphasized the fact that the island had become a place of terror. Fidel Castro also tarnished his reputation by trouble-making in other Latin American countries. Even groups with legitimate grievances against their governments or social systems began to shrink from association with him. Worst of all, Castro firmly placed Cuba in the Communist camp and, in 1962, almost succeeded in making it an offensive base for nuclear missiles aimed at American cities.

How had such a dismaying situation come about? Cuban-American hostility seemed almost unthinkable after the long years of close and mostly cordial association. Had Castro been a Communist fanatic all along, and deceived his own compatriots, intimates, and gullible foreigners? Was he really Cuba's master, or an instrument of the world Communist movement? Or was his commitment unclear even to himself until the United States clumsily alienated him? Was he, perhaps, an authentic nationalist and socialist carrying out a needed revolution that inevitably produced opposition in Cuba and incomprehension abroad? Students of affairs had reached no consensus by 1965. Failure of statesmanship in Havana or Washington, or both, had allowed a completely unexpected situation to develop. Perhaps it would be permanent, perhaps not. In truth, the United States has never quite known what to do about Cuba: whether to let Spain misrule it indefinitely; annex it as a state, like Hawaii; guide it and let it go as an ally, like the Philippines; give it aid and autonomy, like Puerto Rico; or allow it to work out its own destiny and defy Washington for an extended period, only to become a valued partner, like Mexico. This last course would seem to be the most reasonable but for the danger of world Communism irrevocably incorporating the island.

Meanwhile, the success of the revolution after six years was difficult to assess. For the time being, at least, freedom and democracy were banished. Seemingly dedicated reformers had replaced the corrupt politicians who had made the earlier republic a mockery. The status of farm workers, women, and Negroes was probably better. That of the middle classes and urban workingmen was likely worse, and the one-time rich were in exile or stripped. Massive efforts in public education indoctrinated the masses, but illiteracy was sharply reduced and the technological competence of the population elevated. A bold plan to reduce sugar production and diversify agriculture had failed; Cuba's function in the world economy was still to grow as much sugar cane as possible. Nationalization of former plantations had resulted in the creation of state farms, which might or might not be an improvement. Euphoric projects to industrialize the island had, at least temporarily, ended in confusion. It was still problematical whether Cuba could exchange American capital, technology, and commercial ties for those of the Communist bloc and thrive.

A semitropical island with 6,500,000 people and 44,000 square miles, with magnificent agricultural potential, woods, grasslands, and some minerals, Cuba should be an earthly paradise. A benign climate makes it a good place to live, and the popular mood has usually been easygoing. Since 1959 Cuba's rulers have sought to wrench it from its historic bearings. The outcome of this experiment will probably be meaningful for the New World.

THE SPANISH PRESENCE
The Spanish Come, the Indians Go (1492-1700)

Christopher Columbus was the first representative of Western civilization to wax enthusiastic about Cuba. When he discovered the land on October 27, 1492, and explored its northeastern coast for five weeks thereafter, he repeatedly expressed his joyous reaction to its wooded and mountainous beauties, the gentle natives, and the possibilities of wealth. He was undecided whether "Juana," as he named it in honor of the heir of Ferdinand and Isabella, or "Cuba," as the inhabitants were understood to call it, was an island or a peninsula of Asia, but he had no doubt that it was in the Indies. The Discoverer turned eastward to examine the coast of the large island near Cuba— Hispaniola—and to return to Spain. On his second voyage he departed from Hispaniola to spend approximately three months, from April to July 1494, exploring the southern shores of Cuba in the confident expectation that he would soon encounter Oriental potentates. His hopes were unfulfilled, for the fabled wonders of the East refused to appear, but Columbus continued to be enchanted with the semitropical verdure of the country and the friendly Indians who hailed the Spaniards as people from Heaven and offered them bits of gold, cotton, and cigars. After exploring the small islands which he named Gardens of the Queen, Jamaica, and the Isle of Pines, the great admiral at length ended his foray into the west and returned to Hispaniola. Before he left Cuba, however, he had his crew swear that it was not an island but a peninsula, thus hoping to convince his monarchs that he had reached the Asian mainland.

Seventeen years were to pass before the Spaniards returned in force to Cuba. Spain, indeed Europe, quickly recovered from the initial optimism inspired by the return of Columbus from his first voyage. If the lands he had found were in the Indies, they seemed far from the great centers of wealth; in any case they were not particularly productive. In 1500, Juan de la Cosa made a map which showed Cuba, or "Fernandina," as the Spaniards renamed it, an island. Columbus himself spent a short period in the cays of southern Cuba in 1503 when wormy ships forced him to land during his fourth voyage. Finally, in 1508, Sebastián de Ocampo circumnavigated Cuba and proved beyond doubt that it was an island and not a protrusion of Cathay.

By 1511 the Spanish enterprise in the "Indies" included a sound base in Hispaniola and establishments in Puerto Rico, Jamaica, and the northern shore of South America. Interest in Cuba as a source of labor and gold had increased to the point that many individuals coveted the right to conquer it. According to the original agreement between Columbus and the crown, this privilege should have gone to the Discoverer's son, Diego, now governor of Hispaniola and titular viceroy of the Indies; but the crown had been circumscribing the rights of the Columbus family for some time. Credit was given to a prevalent rumor that Diego knew of a huge cache of treasure hidden on Cuba by his father. After much maneuvering, a rich and impressive planter named Diego de Velázquez won the prize, nominally with the approval of Diego but actually through personal channels to King Ferdinand that made him independent of the governor. Velázquez sailed in 1511 with about three hundred men from what is now Haiti and established the first Spanish town in Cuba—Baracoa. His reception was much less friendly than Columbus' had been, since the Cubans had been alerted to the hardships attending Spanish imperialism by refugees from Hispaniola. One of them, a chieftain named Hatuey, caused considerable trouble before he was captured and burned at the stake. This first of Cuba's heroes declared that he did not wish to be converted and go to Heaven, because Christians might be there!

Only two years were required for the able Velázquez and his lieutenants, who included Hernán Cortés and Pánfilo de Narváez of fame later in the conquest of Mexico, to destroy Cuban resistance. Nearly all the conquistadors had been in the New World long enough to employ terroristic methods without qualm. Horses, steel armor plate and swords, crossbows, and gunpowder gave them incontrovertible military advantages. Fierce hounds were highly useful in warning of native ambushes and in scattering opposition, and the employment of ships enabled the Spaniards to sail around geographical obstacles. Harsh as the conquest of Cuba must have been, it was probably as little destructive of life as any the Spaniards were to wage. By 1515, seven Spanish towns had been established: Baracoa, Bayamo, Santiago de Cuba, Puerto Príncipe, Sancti Spiritus, Trinidad, and Havana.

Gold taken from the Indians enabled Diego de Velázquez to ship a very substantial treasure to King Ferdinand in 1515 as the royal fifth to which the crown was customarily entitled, and a much larger payment went in 1517. The governor lieutenant, as Velázquez was known, lost little time in putting the Indians to work sifting gold dust from the streams and scraping it out of the banks. Having been in Hispaniola from 1493 to 1511, Velázquez well knew the importance of building an economic base to support mining. Therefore he introduced grain, vegetables, fruits, and sugar, and he imported cattle and hogs. In order to reward the Spaniards and to obtain their cooperation in making the colony self-supporting, he instituted the *encomienda* system, by which Indian clans were assigned to conquistadors. Probably the method worked well from the standpoint of the Spaniards, most of whom had learned in Hispaniola how to compel natives to labor. It is likely that a few Negro slaves arrived in Cuba about 1515 or soon afterward. With the conquest of Cuba accomplished, considerable gold mined, agriculture and ranching started, and a familiar labor system instituted, the island promised to become a viable colony. Many Spaniards left the peninsula or Hispaniola to make their fortunes in Cuba, their ambitions encouraged by a government that offered them free passage and relief from taxation. As would be true on many occasions in the future, Cuba's destiny was not to be so easily predictable. The natives could not adapt to the oppressive system imposed upon them. Their island paradise disorganized by the Spanish conquest, they had neither incentive nor the ability to engage in long hours of gold-washing and farming for the benefit of the invader. Many died from overwork and cruelty; many were massacred as they sought to escape; most by far died from diseases brought by the European. As had happened in Hispaniola, the native race declined at a shocking rate. In Cuba a defender of the Indians arose among the invaders, Bartolomé de Las Casas, one of the very few Spaniards to be honored throughout Latin America. A one-time conquistador who was perhaps the first Christian clergyman to be ordained in the New World, Las Casas arrived with the Velázquez expedition as a Dominican friar. Soon after he reached Cuba an overwhelming religious experience caused him to speak up for the natives. He returned to Spain in 1515, along with the first shipment of gold. Strangely, Las Casas' tales of Indian suffering had more impact than the treasure, at least on the mind of the regent, Cardinal Francisco Ximenes de Cisneros. Yet the elaborate system the friar and the cardinal worked out to save the Indians had little effect but to redeem in part Spain's reputation with posterity. Mainly because of Spanish-borne germs, the native population died out so steadily that perhaps only five thousand were left in Cuba by the middle of the sixteenth century.

Meanwhile, Velázquez inadvertently contributed to the destruction of his colony by sending sea expeditions to the mainland. A voyage to Yucatan in 1517 brought information about the Maya centers and rumors of still greater wonders. In 1518 Velázquez' nephew, Juan de Grijalva, explored the Mexican coast further and sent back word of fabulous cities in the interior. That same year Velázquez organized a massive expedition and requested permission from Spain to send it into the rumored kingdoms in central Mexico. But before his authorization arrived, the captain of this expedition,

Hernán Cortés, sailed away against Velázquez' orders and eventually conquered the Aztecs. Having lost perhaps seven hundred Spaniards through this treachery, Velázquez gathered a larger force to apprehend Cortés and to bring Mexico under his control. But this army, which was led by Pánfilo de Narváez, also succumbed to Cortés' wiles and skill, and Velázquez was left to console himself as best he could for humiliation, a lost fortune, and the ruin of his thriving colony.

Cuba was indeed ruined, so much so that she did not recover for generations. The spotlight of destiny had played briefly on the island before shifting to Mexico and, later, to Peru. Hundreds of Spaniards had come into Cuba to build a society under Velázquez, only to be lured to the far greater opportunities on the mainland. Towns, farms, ranches, and mines were deserted, leaving only a residue of the weaker and more timid inhabitants to do what they could with the wreckage. The exodus of the dynamic element, however, failed to benefit the natives, who were disappearing so rapidly that nothing could save them. It was symptomatic of Velázquez' decline in state that Diego Columbus came to Cuba in 1522, to assert his authority briefly, and that he and other officials were able to prosecute Velázquez for real and alleged failures. The conqueror died in 1524.

So downgraded was Cuba by then that the crown allowed it to revert to the control of the Columbus family until 1536, when they sold their rights. Several lieutenant governors came and went; all apparently had friction with the remaining colonists and with their superiors in Hispaniola. Santiago de Cuba was now the capital, replacing Baracoa, though Havana was becoming the major town because it was on the direct sea route from Mexico to Spain. It looked for a time as though the municipalities might achieve a representative government for the island. In each town the Spaniards chose a council or *cabildo* to govern the settlement and its surrounding area. Once a year procurators went from each council to Santiago de Cuba to draw up petitions to the crown and to confer on common problems. Inevitably, they disputed with the lieutenant governors or the high court (*audiencia*) in Hispaniola. Probably because Charles V had a frightening experience with municipal defiance in Spain, he eventually forbade these annual assemblies. After this, town government in Cuba tended to decline, as it did everywhere throughout the

Spanish empire. Nor did the ecclesiastical establishment do much to buttress law and authority. The secular clergy was small and ineffective in many ways, and the few Franciscan and Dominican friars tended to be targets of criticism on grounds of misbehavior.

The departure of most of the Spaniards for the mainland permitted the Indians to strike for freedom sporadically. Two waves of pestilence, however, in 1519 and 1528, further reduced their numbers. In 1525-29 the crown attempted to enforce humane legislation by congregating Indians in communities ruled by clergymen. But the friars colluded with the settlers, and these half-hearted experiments only hastened the decline of the natives. The last general native uprising occurred in 1529, when one Guama led a rebellion. As usual, the whites defeated it. In 1531 the crown ordered that no further enslavements take place and in 1532 that deserving Indians be freed, but the settlers paid scant attention to humanitarian commands from Spain. It was already clear that Africans, who were stronger and more advanced than Indians, were to provide a labor force as rapidly as the Spaniards in Cuba could purchase them.

Some stabilization had been attained in 1538 in spite of the tragedies of the Indians and the demoralization of the whites. In that year, Hernando de Soto arrived as governor of Cuba and, unfortunately, *adelantado** of Florida, which had proved a graveyard of previous Spanish expeditions. De Soto brought with him so many warriors and ships that he at first terrified the inhabitants of Santiago de Cuba, who feared a foreign conquest; he recruited white settlers until he had an expedition of six hundred for the effort in what is now the southern part of the United States. In 1539 he transferred the seat of government to Havana and sailed away, leaving his wife Isabel in charge. Not until 1543 did Doña Isabel learn that she was a widow and that the expedition had been a fiasco.

Another period of desolation followed. Perhaps only six or seven hundred white settlers were left in Cuba, along with a few hundred Negroes and possibly five thousand Indians. Some consternation arose with the publication of the New Laws in 1544, which provided for the end of the *encomienda* system at the death of the present holders. The partial withdrawal of the New Laws caused relief, but in 1552 the crown ordered that all Indians be liberated. Perhaps some of

* Ruler of a frontier province or prospective conqueror of new territory.

them were. In any event, Cuban Indians were almost extinct, and the strain of aboriginal blood in modern Cubans must be infinitesimal.

The government of the island continued to be unedifying and yet, as was true generally during the reign of Philip II (1556-98), it gradually hardened into the monolithic pattern that made Spanish imperialism authoritative and regularized. It is difficult to ascertain whether the governors were all dishonest, or whether their superiors were, or whether the crown was unreasonably suspicious. In any case, they suffered many hardships. Governors usually resided in Havana, where they were not welcome because they interfered in municipal and personal affairs. Their terms were short and ended with the inevitable *residencia*, an inquest in which aggrieved subjects and skeptical royal accountants examined their activities while in office. Often the former governors served time in prison, sometimes under the most brutal conditions, and had to pay huge fines for misdeeds. Yet they somehow made good the will of the king to rule the island and to be feared. In time they usurped most of the powers claimed by the municipalities. Something was salvaged when a *visitador* (inspector) named Alonso de Cáceres removed a governor in 1574 and issued ordinances that preserved some powers of the town councils, among them the regulation of slave conditions and the right to award land titles, both of which had much to do with the eventual development of a colonial society.

Patterns of the Mid-Colonial Period

Cuba's true destiny in world affairs has been to serve as a base of strategic importance. This was suggested in the mid-sixteenth century, after the Spaniards regularized the sea traffic from the Americas. Earlier, Cortés had sent his first shipment from Mexico by the sea lane between Cuba and the Florida keys. The value of this route was at once apparent: ships could stop in Havana for supplies, then pass through the channel between Florida and the Bahamas via the Gulf Stream and utilize that current for a fast voyage to Spain. Treasures taken from the Aztecs and later the Incas, and then the vast silver extractions from Mexican and Peruvian mines, went on sailing vessels that used this route. Dangers from foreign enemies made it prudent for the ships to sail in convoy, which was the usual practice by the 1540s. As early as 1538 a French fleet had occupied Havana, in 1554 a pirate called Peg-Leg Leclerc seized Santiago de Cuba, and in 1555 another corsair, Jacques de Sores, a Lutheran, burned Havana.

Pedro Menéndez de Avilés played a major role in organizing the Spanish fleet system with Havana as its crucial component. Arriving in 1565 as *adelantado* of Florida, he massacred a small colony of French Huguenots and established St. Augustine. Since the governor of Cuba did not cooperate with him, Menéndez had him removed and secured his own appointment in 1567. A strong ruler, he furthered the fortification of Havana and established the stores and supplies needed to make it the chief naval base in Spain's overseas empire. According to his scheme, which operated until 1778, homebound ships from Panama and Mexico effected a rendezvous in Havana to be fitted for the trans-Atlantic voyage. Nearly every year, after the hurricane season, a monster fleet, well-guarded by warships and carrying bullion, passengers, mail, and a few colonial raw materials, would depart for Spain. During the more than two centuries that this system operated, only one entire convoy was lost, and the attrition of others was much smaller than might be expected.

The fleet system brought new importance to Havana, which formally became the capital of Cuba in 1589 and which was elevated to the rank of city (*ciudad*) in 1594. A fort known as the *Fuerza*, which is probably the oldest European structure in the New World to remain in use, was finally completed, and the famous *Morro* and *Punta* castles were built on each side of the harbor mouth. Construction workers and substantial garrisons needed to guard these fortifications added to Havana's population. And as crews from the fleets and passengers of all types lingered in the city, often for months at a time, facilities developed to lodge and feed them and to cater to their pleasures. Furthermore, most of the vessels required repair and supplies before undertaking the long voyage to Spain. Hence technicians, slaves and unskilled white workers, and vendors were in abundance. The city had its peculiar character. Cramped, dirty, smelly, and colorful, it huddled behind the coastal fortifications and, by the middle of the seventeenth century, within walls to its rear. Ditches brought in water, but sewage and garbage were rarely removed. The population habitually gouged the transients, who themselves often behaved with holiday abandon or criminal rowdiness, and the moral tone of Havana was, and has remained, low.

The tawdry atmosphere of Havana reflected not only the nature of its economic base but also an unwise command arrangement. The governor, or captain-general as he was usually called after 1580, was the ranking officer in the island, but he had no authority over the crews from the ships, who answered to the fleet commander. And garrisons who manned the castles were under the governor of the *Fuerza*. Jealousies among these officers permitted crime and excessively spirited behavior to go unpunished, a situation which the sailors and soldiers exploited. That the divided command was not only administratively untidy but potentially dangerous became clear in 1586, when a large English armada captained by Sir Francis Drake hovered off Havana for some days before electing not to attack. Soon after this fright, Governor Juan Tejada wrung from Philip II the right to exercise supreme authority over Havana. Although conditions then improved somewhat, the city continued to be a center of vice, gambling, crime, and prostitution. It even attracted delinquents who were not wanted in Spain or the mainland colonies.

The death of Philip II in 1598 marked a downward turning point in nearly every section of the far-flung Spanish monarchy, though the decline of Spain itself had really set in sooner. Except for Havana, Cuba had scant value as a colony, and for most of the seventeenth century it contributed so little to the royal treasury that subsidies from the Viceroyalty of New Spain (Mexico) were necessary to meet its expenses. Officials of both the government and the Church were often inept, incompetent, and corrupt. In 1607 the island was divided into two units, with a captain-general in Havana and an autonomous captain or governor in Santiago de Cuba. The area between these cities was largely ungoverned, consisting of grasslands and woods inhabited by a few ranchers and their hands, or by contrabandists and escaped slaves known as *cimarrones*. There was an archbishop in Santiago de Cuba who was nominally in control of the ecclesiastical establishment, but the secular clergy was very small and even the regular orders were few in number and active mainly in operating a handful of monasteries and several schools. The famous Spanish bureaucratic structure that governed Mexico and Peru with such style and prestige (though often not very well) had only a pale counterpart in Cuba.

Seventeenth-century economic activities in Cuba centered mostly about contraband, a reflection of the frail governmental establishment. Thousands of foreign enemies and outlaws cruised about the Caribbean seeking opportunities to exchange slaves and finished goods for hides, fresh meat, and timber whenever there was nothing to loot, as was usually the case in Cuba. The island had far too many harbors to be policed, and officials usually connived in smuggling when they were involved at all. The town of Bayamo become the unofficial headquarters for the contrabandists. Far enough from the sea to be safe from seizure, its tough inhabitants utilized the Cauto River to effect contacts with foreign traders. The game went on for generations, until by the close of the century sand bars formed in the stream and spoiled the easy entrance and egress. In other localities colonial Cubans enjoyed years of uninterrupted trading with pirates and national enemies.

Among legal economic activities, business at Havana went on rather steadily, despite the smaller fleets and the long periods of blockade during the seventeenth century, when Spain's enemies dominated the coasts. Copper production, which had begun at El Cobre mine near Santiago de Cuba in 1530, gradually assumed enough importance to be a significant export. Most of it, however, went into local use for making bells and cooking utensils. As the smoking and snuff-taking habit spread over Europe, Cuban tobacco acquired a minor place in filling the market, particularly after 1629, when a governor began a steady trade by shipping some of the commodity to the Canary Islands. Cuba's woods, some of which were very fine and prized enough to be included in building the Escorial fortress-monastery, were used in shipbuilding and repair in Havana and occasionally for export. Livestock raising was common all over the island; the herds, having multiplied since the days of Velázquez, were roaming unclaimed over lands that were also largely unclaimed, until bands of horsemen caught them for hides and meat. Almost any kind of fruit or vegetable could be raised, but consumption was local except for sales to seamen, Spanish or other.

A beginning was apparent in what would be Cuba's pride, or tragedy—sugarcane cultivation. The crop had been grown for home use

since the earliest days of the Spanish presence; a group of *habaneros*
secured from Philip II soon before he died a grant of funds to con-
struct a sugar mill near the capital. The experiment was highly successful, for Cuba, like the other islands of the Antilles, had precisely
the right conditions for producing sugar. The cane required little
care, since it grew year after year without replanting. During the
cutting season, however, a frenzy of effort was needed to remove
the stalks and to crush them while still fresh. So voracious was the
European market that production grew steadily, and by the end of
the seventeenth century perhaps one hundred sugar mills, operated
by human or animal labor, were functioning. African labor was regarded as essential during the critical cutting and processing season,
and slaves were imported as rapidly as Cubans could afford them.
Hence sugarcane raising, often regarded as a curse by Caribbean
historians, began to reshape the economy of the island and to establish new social patterns.

Events during the seventeenth century were usually of a violent
nature, such as assaults by foreigners and pirates. In 1603 an outlaw
named Gilberto Girón sacked Santiago de Cuba and attempted to
conquer Bayamo. The capture of an entire Spanish treasure fleet by
the Dutch admiral, Piet Heyn, off Matanzas in 1628 was one of the
most sensational occurrences of the century. Several long-lasting
blockades of Havana and incursions by enemies into other ports
kept the island in a state of uneasiness. England's conquest of
Jamaica had evil consequences for Cuba. In 1662 the new neighbors
robbed and burned Santiago de Cuba. With French allies they returned in 1665 to take Sancti Spiritus. More fearful than English
and French regular forces were the outlaws, who by mid-century
established a headquarters in Tortuga, an island off northern Haiti,
and in Jamaica. The notorious Welshman, Henry Morgan, sacked
Puerto Príncipe in 1668, and his followers molested Cuban settlements intermittently until the end of the century. The Isle of Pines
and the string of islands on the south coast known as the Queen's
Gardens were especially suitable as bases for pirates. Cuba was quite
vulnerable to such characters, but her poverty deterred frequent attacks. Even so, a tradition of violence and constant apprehension of
danger became part of Cuba's heritage. Her development lagged,
and after two centuries of Spanish civilization she was still a primi-

tive land. During the dreary seventeenth century the population was believed to have increased from 30,000 to about 60,000.

An Age of Regeneration and Revolution (1700-1814)

The accession of the French Bourbons to the throne of Spain in 1700 inaugurated not only the War of the Spanish Succession (1701-14) but also a multitude of reforms both in the peninsula and the overseas empire. The war brought a boom to Havana, since the French fleet anchored there for extended periods and the city served as a base for Franco-Spanish assaults on English possessions. Cuba suffered little, though English corsairs sacked Trinidad in 1702 and large fleets threatened Havana on several occasions. The Bourbons and their numerous French advisers almost from the first created a new mood in the desultory Spanish empire. Integrity and zeal were now prized in officials, hacks were replaced, and inefficiency scorned. For most of the eighteenth century Cuba had rulers of ability who, even if they were despotic and overly attentive to revenue collection, usually carried out their duties competently.

With the war over, the royal authorities undertook in 1715 to consolidate tobacco production in Cuba so as to increase sales and revenues. A monopoly company known as the *Factoria* was established to purchase all Cuban tobacco at fixed prices and to handle its sale abroad. This early example of state capitalism, to be repeated so often in twentieth-century Latin America, caused much distress among the small tobacco raisers, or *vegueros,* most of whom were in the Havana area. It was obvious that the monopoly was not concerned with their welfare but with profits, and that it intended to buy cheap and sell dear. In 1717 the *vegueros* organized machete-wielding bands to keep the *Factoria* agents out of the tobacco country. Emboldened by their success, they congregated in Havana and so humiliated the captain-general that he resigned. His replacement, General Gregorio Guazo, led a thousand soldiers and horsemen into the countryside and hunted down the leading rebels, many of whom were hanged. To be sure, the *vegueros* protested their loyalty to the king; all they opposed, they said, was bad government; and probably they were sincere. After crushing the movement entirely, by 1723, the government heeded some of the complaints and made concessions. The *Factoria* continued to be unpopular with the tobacco growers, and possibly it harmed the industry, but it lasted until 1817. Another monopoly company, the *Real Compañía de Comercio* was created in 1740 to handle all imports and exports in Havana. It too acquired a bad reputation among Cubans, who felt that they were being fleeced and that commerce was restricted in order to keep prices high.

Cultural life began to flicker under the Bourbons. Early in the century Bishop Diego Evelino de Compostela publicly shamed the clergy for its lassitude in welfare work, and he invigorated educational and charitable agencies. The College of San Francisco de Sales and the Seminary of San Ambrosio began to function with some effectiveness. In 1720 the first press went into operation, printing official notices and shipping news. Not until 1764 was there a regular newspaper. The University of San Jerónimo in Havana was opened in 1728, a mark of prestige for a Spanish colony though it had few students, professors, or books. The beginning of the cathedral of Havana in 1748 and many other public buildings, as well as finer homes built for the wealthy, attested to the solid if somewhat delayed growth of Cuba.

Great Britain was Spain's most dangerous foe in the eighteenth century. Following the end of the long War of the Spanish Succession were years of disputes and occasional hostilities resulting from Britain's abuse of the *asiento*, or license to import slaves into the Spanish empire, and her pressures to break the Spanish commercial monopoly. The War of Jenkins' Ear (a conflict between Britain and Spain growing out of disputes regarding commerce and command of the Caribbean Sea), which merged into the War of the Austrian Succession, made the Caribbean a danger zone from 1739 to 1748. Cuba had more importance than ever as a strategic center, serving as Spain's prime naval base and staging area for assaults on British possessions. The formidable British commander, Admiral Vernon, occupied Guantánamo in 1740 and threatened both Havana and Santiago de Cuba with huge forces. Spain survived these and other dangers, but the British grasped that Havana truly was, as its title stated, the "key to the New World and bulwark of the Indies," and they planned to capture it in any future conflict.

The opportunity came after Charles III of Spain foolishly entered the Seven Years' War in its last stages, against Britain. In 1762 a force of 200 warships and transports and 25,000 redcoats under the command of Lord Albemarle disembarked in the vicinity of Havana. The Spanish had about 4,000 regulars and 10,000 volunteers to meet the threat. After a siege of forty-four days, which involved shelling the city and mining the *Morro*, Albemarle occupied it, to remain for almost a year, to July 1763. Spanish resistance was strong enough to prevent the conquest of any significant territory beyond Havana. As governor, Albemarle hoped to persuade the Cubans to switch their allegiance to Great Britain and to make his rule palatable by proclaiming religious toleration, free trade, and many civil liberties as well as the continuation of the traditional administration under British direction. The colonists did not respond to his conciliatory approach. They were loyal Spaniards and would not be tempted. Yet the British occupation brought so many changes that some Cubans claim that the history of their country really begins with 1762. Most pleasing of all was the burst of commercial activity. From the half-dozen ships a year permitted by the monopoly company, the total rose to almost a thousand under the British. Slaves and European goods poured into the port, and exports spurted. Havana (along with Manila, which the British had also occupied) was restored to Spain by the peace treaty, in exchange for Florida and the Bahama Islands. Soon afterward, Louis XV ceded to Charles III his claims to Louisiana west of the Mississippi and to New Orleans.

Things were never the same afterward. Too many *habaneros* had seen what profits might come their way if they traded freely with the British, and Spain did not dare to restore the monopoly company. Wisely, the crown sought to placate Cuban colonials by awarding them titles of nobility, providing better administration, and making Havana virtually impregnable to invasion. So formidable were the rebuilt fortifications that the city has not to this day been taken from the outside. Cuban pride was flattered by the attachment of Louisiana to its jurisdiction, which had to be effected in 1769 by a large expeditionary force from Havana. The establishment in 1764 of the intendant system, already so successful in Spain, centralized and improved administration in Cuba. Of considerable importance in strengthening the captain-general was the continuation of a right, won during days of emergency during wartime, of appointing a military commander to defend towns. This official practically superseded the municipal governments. Like most of the Bourbon innovations, this one resulted in rule that was more honest and efficient, but also more autocratic.

Remarkable progress followed the Seven Years' War. Cuba's population grew rapidly, reaching 171,000 according to the census of 1774, with whites numbering 96,000, Negro slaves 44,000, and mixed-blooded persons 31,000. Coffee was introduced as a cash crop in 1768, to flourish in several parts of the island and to produce significant profits and revenues. When Florida passed to Britain, some of its Spanish inhabitants removed to Cuba and set up a thriving business selling beeswax. Although tobacco had long had commercial value, its importance increased, particularly after it was discovered that the westernmost, and hitherto neglected, province of Pinar del Río had choice lands for its cultivation. Despite the complaints about the *Factoria*'s high-handedness, tobacco production was socially beneficial because it strengthened small farmers and imbued a pride in patient craftsmanship in making cigars. Livestock probably remained the most important economic activity in the island, but sugarcane raising developed very rapidly. By 1790 perhaps 500 *ingenios* (small sugar mills) were functioning, mostly in the central sections of the island. Furthermore, commerce flourished after the British occupation, particularly when, in 1778, the crown opened most ports in the peninsula and Spanish America to trade with one another. In the following year, thanks to Spanish aid to the American Revolution, Havana was allowed to trade freely with the rebellious English colonies and often with French possessions in the Caribbean. The crown's revenues accordingly waxed, and so did the Cuban economy.

The captain-generals of the eighteenth century, as noted, were ordinarily capable. Among the best remembered was the Marquis de la Torre, who reigned during the period of the American Revolution and presided over the boom in Cuban commerce, and who supervised the Spanish campaign in Florida which resulted in the return of that province to Spain, and to Cuba's jurisdiction, in 1783. It was also a period of much public and private construction in the rococo style in Havana, which acquired a theater, paved and lighted streets, and homes handsome enough to gratify the wealthy. The rise in urban values was pronounced, but it was almost equaled by the enhanced land price in rural areas. Most of the island was by now occupied, and it became important for the first time for ranchers and planters to assert their land titles to tracts that had been awarded to them—as was often done prior to 1729—by the various municipal councils, but that had lain dormant for many years.

Perhaps the most gratefully remembered captain-general was Luis de Las Casas, who reigned from 1790 to 1796. Personally popular and identified with the nascent nationalism of creoles, the white persons born in the New World, he also sponsored the liberalism which was becoming fashionable among educated Cubans. He successfully opposed a bishop who tried to censor public entertainments and he encouraged the press, which suddenly spawned several regular newspapers. He also received credit for liberalism in commerce: Spain was at war with Revolutionary France in 1793-95 and therefore allowed Cuba to trade with Britain and the United States. And when Spain and Britain went to war in 1796, Cuba continued trade with the United States and reopened trade with France. An event of lasting significance was the establishment in 1792 of the Royal Economic Society of Friends of the Country, one of many such organizations of professional and business men and planters in the Spanish world. A branch had been set up in Santiago de Cuba even prior to the one in Havana. The latter was destined to serve as a focus of economic liberalism among the upper classes for most of the nineteenth century, as well as a political center and a cultural stimulus. And in 1795 a so-called *consulado* of Agriculture and Commerce was created by the crown to promote the economic well-being of the colony. Its first syndic was a remarkable creole named Francisco de Arango y Parreño, who long represented Cuban interests in Madrid with great success.

The ferment of the 1790s reflected both the French Revolution and a considerable official enlightenment in Spain during the dominance of Manuel Godoy, the favorite of Charles IV. Cuba's economy boomed as never before because of the new vigor. It was, furthermore, greatly stimulated by the disaster that befell the French colonies, particularly Saint-Domingue (Haiti), when the slaves rose up and destroyed the sugar industry. Perhaps 30,000 French refugees fled to Cuba, often bringing with them their skilled mulatto labor. In many cases they went back into the sugar business, introducing improved methods of crushing cane with overshot water mills, closed furnaces, and other techniques. Most of Haiti's fabulous sugar market was now open to Cuba. And the United States was rapidly becoming a voracious customer of Caribbean sugar. The very sharp rise in the price of sugar that accompanied these developments caused many Cubans to plunge heavily into the industry. Great tracts of land went into cane cultivation, and mills were constructed. Slave labor was urgently required. Since Negroes who had been exposed to rebellion in other colonies were not wanted, Africa was necessarily the source. Arango demonstrated his usefulness to Cuban creoles by obtaining permission in Spain for the unlimited importation of human cargoes, and thousands were brought in.

On a lesser scale the coffee industry experienced a similar boom. The ruin of France's colonial production was to Cuba's advantage. On the other hand, tobacco suffered a slump because the British blockade of the continent cut off the market for Cuban cigars. While prices occasionally fell as fast as they had risen, massive economic growth was the basic condition of Cuba for a generation after the beginning of the French Revolution. Cubans spoke of the times as "the fat cows" or "the thin cows," depending on how prosperous they had been in a given year. Certainly the fat cows predominated during the era that saw so much of Europe in convulsion. Developments in the New World also had sharp effects on Cuba. After Spain ceded Santo Domingo to France by the Peace of Basle in 1795, the ancient *audiencia* of that colony was transferred to Puerto Príncipe. The archbishopric of Santo Domingo removed to Santiago de Cuba. And although Spaniards and Dominicans maintain that the wrong ashes were disinterred, Cubans received the supposed remains of Christopher Columbus. When Haitian Negroes overran Santo Domingo in 1801, thousands of Spaniards fled to Cuba. Other Spaniards, and many Frenchmen too, came to Cuba from New Orleans when Louisiana was sold to the United States in 1803.

The Marquis of Someruelos reigned as captain-general from 1799 to 1812, a period of erratic prosperity and revolution. A prudent and yet vigorous ruler, he won the support of the creoles by suppressing slave unrest while at the same time encouraging African forced immigration. He also pleased the Cubans by keeping the ports open to world commerce even when Madrid ordered otherwise. A crisis of unprecedented magnitude broke upon the Spanish empire in 1808, when Napoleon forcibly substituted his brother Joseph Bonaparte for the Bourbons on the throne, thereby initiating a political disintegration from which the Spanish world has never recovered. In Havana, the peninsular and creole leaders pondered their course with a commendable spirit of conciliation and responsibility. Like Spanish subjects everywhere, they refused to accept the Bonaparte king. The only issue was whether Cuba should govern itself through a provisional junta under Someruelos or place itself under a supreme junta in Sevilla that was asserting its right to rule in the absence of the Bourbon monarch, Ferdinand VII, then interned in France. Someruelos tactfully kept peninsular-creole tension from obtruding and steered the leaders into accepting, and keeping, the second course. Cuba remained loyal to the absent king and those who professed to speak for him, and avoided the turbulence that soon beset most of the Spanish empire in America.

Cuba's fidelity to Ferdinand VII during his captivity from 1808 to 1814, and after he returned to the throne, was attributable only partially to the skill of Someruelos and his successors. The island was full of peninsulars, who had a strong group spirit which social clubs nourished and who in 1811 organized a militia called the Volunteers. Many were merchants and officials, but the most important were the military forces, for Cuba had long been the major Spanish base in America. Rebellion would have been very difficult. Nor was the spirit of rebellion strong. Unlike the long-established creole mining and planter aristocracies of the mainland colonies, who were often quick to defy peninsular authority, the affluent creole class in Cuba was just now coming into its own. Since their new prosperity was based on Negro slavery, they were fearful of doing anything to weaken the government lest an uprising of the Haitian type occur. Few of them were educated enough to be stirred by the revolutionary thought that inspired their equivalents in Venezuela, Bogotá, Mexico, or Buenos Aires.

Thus there was little agitation in Cuba when, in August 1810, two creole deputies were elected to the Spanish *Cortes* at Cádiz that was called to preserve the sovereignty of the monarchy. This body proved to be surprisingly radical, proclaiming the Constitution of 1812 and many human rights and economic liberties. It authorized

Cuba to elect deputations or legislatures for each of its three provinces and members of the municipal councils, to raise a creole militia, and to enjoy most of the freedoms associated with the American and French Revolutions. While this taste of representative government was pleasing to many Cuban creoles—and would not be forgotten—the more influential among them were nervous about the radicalism of the *Cortes*, its attacks on the Church, and most of all, indications that it might abolish Negro slavery. The threat of this last passed, probably with the help of bribes, and in any case the Constitution of 1812 was outlawed and the *Cortes* disbanded when Ferdinand returned in 1814.

Cubans gave little indication of being inspired by the liberal period or offended by its termination. Only the most obscure plots and rumors had disturbed the authorities during these years. General James Wilkinson appears to have sounded out the Spanish governor of Florida in behalf of President Jefferson in 1809 on the possibility of promoting a break of that province and Cuba from Spanish rule. In 1810-11 another American agent, William Shaler, secretly discussed with a few Cubans the course that might be followed should the *Cortes* abolish slavery or Great Britain seek to gain the island. Soon the United States had a war of its own with Britain, and, if it had ever entertained any serious designs on Cuba, had to drop them. Of local trouble-makers there were surprisingly few between 1808 and 1814. A Mexican Bonapartist, Manuel Rodríguez Alemán, plotted mischief and was executed in Cuba. Two republicans were known to be active. One was caught and killed; the other, Joaquín Infante, escaped to Venezuela and devised a constitution for a free Cuba. The worst scare was caused by a free mulatto, José Antonio Aponte, who was executed with eight others for conspiring to bring about a slave revolt.

Uneasy Colonial Status (1814-1868)

The efforts of Ferdinand VII and his absolutist regime to mollify the American subjects who had displayed so much disaffection during his absence were only temporarily successful in the mainland empire. It was different with Cuba, partly because of her loyal record, which won her the title, "ever-faithful isle," and partly because of Francisco de Arango. Now a member of the Council of Indies in Madrid,

Arango drafted many plans for improving the American empire, a few of which won approval. He secured the abolition of the *Factoria*, or tobacco monopoly, in 1817. In 1818 he obtained for Cuba the right to allow foreign ships to enter her ports almost without restriction. And in 1819 he won royal authorization to legalize titles to lands awarded to individuals by municipalities prior to 1729, when they were curbed in this practice. The census of 1817 illustrated the growth of the island. Now there were 552,000 inhabitants, 239,000 of them whites. Although the nonwhite population of 313,000 was expanding faster, a treaty of 1817 which Great Britain forced on Ferdinand VII called for the cessation of the slave trade by 1820, and thus indicated an end to the progressive Africanization of Cuba.

Spain underwent a second experience with the Constitution of 1812 when it came back into force between 1820 and 1823, a period that alienated conservatives in the American empire and hastened the independence of the mainland colonies. In Cuba the captain-general swore to uphold the constitution as ordered by Madrid and local radicals, most of whom were peninsular Spaniards, usually low-ranking officers and shopkeepers. For some time they worked through secret lodges and public demonstrations to build up democratic sentiment. Cuban creoles, on the other hand, tended to be wary of liberalism but were becoming far more receptive to ideas of independence. Some of this interest stemmed from disgust with Spain, the crude absolutism of Ferdinand VII from 1814 to 1820, and the antics of the radicals in 1820-23. Furthermore, the liberating movements led by San Martín in southern South America, Bolívar in the northern part of that continent, Pedro I in Brazil, and Iturbide in Mexico also inspired a few Cubans. And then there were occasional native radicals, such as Father Félix Varela, a popular teacher at the seminary who taught students to think in political terms and to apply Christian justice to social problems. A young officer, José Francisco Lemus, and a poet, José María Heredia, organized a secret society in 1823 named the "Suns and Rays of Bolívar" to plan rebellion and union with the famed Liberator. Plots and the ventilation of advanced ideas were not the most important aspects of the constitutional period, however. More significant was the widening of the cleavage between creoles and peninsulars. In 1822 tension between these groups caused a street battle in Havana in which *vivas* for independence were sounded.

Thanks to the large French army that occupied Spain in 1823 in the name of the Holy Alliance, Ferdinand VII was restored to absolute power. By that time Cuba was one of the few provinces in America still loyal to Spain, and the crown applied energetic measures to rid it of radicals or advocates of independence. Many emigrated, though the Suns and Rays of Bolívar continued to function secretly for a time. There was still some hope that rebels could obtain aid from Bolívar or Mexico, but all of the attempted risings were fiascos or tragedies. Cuba was much too full of peninsular troops and refugees from liberated areas to offer much prospect of revolution. Nor was the United States inclined to smile on Cuban insurrectionists, chiefly because of fear that Great Britain would seize the island if Spanish power were broken. This consideration may have played a part in the announcement of the Monroe Doctrine in December 1823 and in the discouragement by the United States of efforts to liberate Cuba planned for discussion at the Panama Congress of 1826. Spain, of course, had no intention of facilitating either British or American acquisition of the island; rather, she planned to use it as a base for the reconquest of Mexico and other revolted areas. In the hope of strengthening the captain-general's authority to deal with subversion, the king issued the notorious decree of May 28, 1825, which gave the captain-general power to declare a state of siege, to suspend any law or order, and to exile anyone he chose.

Cuba continued to grow rapidly. Former officials of the lost mainland empire, soldiers, and royalists of various sorts poured into the island. Spain cheated on the treaty of 1817 regarding the end of the slave trade, and many Africans continued to be imported. In 1827 the census recorded a population of 704,000, of whom 311,000 were white, 286,000 slaves, and 106,000 free Negroes or mixed bloods. It also listed 1,000 sugar mills, 30,090 ranches, 5,534 tobacco farms, and 2,067 coffee plantations—a surprisingly wide distribution of property that showed how far Cuba was from suffering excessive concentration of wealth. Yet the trends that would make latifundia the prevailing system were in evidence. Sugarcane growing was steadily increasing, having rallied from a few bleak years of "thin cows" caused by the competition of European beet sugar developed during the Napoleonic period. The introduction of steam-driven machinery for the sugar mills in 1819 and other technical improvements brought earlier by refugees from revolutionized lands pointed toward eventual capitalization of the industry. Ranching was gradually losing its primacy to sugar, and Brazil's burgeoning coffee production would soon drive Cuba's coffee farmers out of business and bring about further emphasis on sugarcane.

The disputed succession of the child-queen Isabel II to the throne of Spain in 1833 had strange consequences for Cuba. Although Isabel's supporters against the claims of her absolutist uncle, Don Carlos, proclaimed liberalism and constitutional government, Cuba found itself more oppressed than ever. Spanish liberals looked upon Cuban creoles as slavers and separatists and therefore chose to keep them in hand. The captain-general they appointed in 1834, Miguel Tacón, had fought against the independence cause in South America and had no intention of losing again. Almost from the first he adopted a harsh tone, snubbing the creoles as though they were all subversives, even the respected and loyal Arango. Cuban society had always been centered in the captain-general's palace. Now the creoles broke away and communed with themselves. The overbearing Tacón did accomplish a great deal in a constructive way, despite his unpopularity and bad reputation in Cuba. He started roads, almost the first in the island, supported the beginning of the first railroad, built the famous Prado boulevard and a theater in Havana that bears his name, and waged an energetic campaign against gamblers, thieves, vagabonds, and stray dogs. Systems of garbage disposal and sanitation, spurred by the great cholera epidemic that swept the New World in those years, were other achievements.

In 1836, when the regent of Spain was forced to proclaim the Constitution of 1812, Tacón refused to honor that much-used document. When a general in command of Santiago de Cuba obeyed Madrid and not Tacón, a civil war nearly developed. Soon, however, Tacón removed that officer and proceeded to punish soldiers and officials alike who had in good faith taken an oath to the constitution. Tacón did not interfere with the election of four deputies from Cuba to the revived *Cortes* in Spain, but he pulled wires in Madrid to see that they were not seated. The insult to Cuba by the

Cortes was never forgiven. The reason for the action appeared unconvincing: that Cuba was not really a province of Spain but a possession governed by special laws, including the hated decree of 1825. Spanish liberals further taunted the Cubans by reminding them that they owned slaves and could not expect to enjoy liberties they denied to others.

Tacón ruled on, heedless of the offenses resented by the insulars. He extended the powers of military commissions that took over criminal cases from the *audiencia* at Puerto Príncipe. Possibly because that high court protested, he set in motion the creation of a more pliable *audiencia* at Havana, which was organized after he departed. Tacón freely used his power to exile men. The most remembered victim was José Antonio Saco, who had succeeded Father Varela as the mentor for academic youths and whose influence was, and would remain until his death in 1879, on the side of moderation.

By the time Tacón left Cuba, in 1838, the creole aristocracy had developed considerable group feeling and was critical of Spain. These families drew their wealth mainly from the rural areas, from sugarcane cultivation and ranching, and usually resided there except for social seasons in Havana. They now had enjoyed money long enough to know how to live in style and to appreciate education; hence their sons were likely to go to the United States for schooling. Literary romanticism, which had burst upon Spain suddenly in 1833 with the easing of censorship and was now affecting Cuba, often stimulated political interests in this class, usually in the way of making independence seem attractive. Railroad construction, which was modernizing parts of the island and furthering the concentration of sugar lands into vast estates, promised more wealth and progress. The secularization of Church lands, dictated by the Spanish liberals, also tended to promote the accumulation of property by those who already owned a great deal. Rising in wealth and pretensions, the bolder creoles looked with more and more favor on attaching themselves to the United States. Britain was now unpopular, for she had abolished slavery in her colonies in 1832, and there was no further interest in exchanging Spanish for British rule. But the United States was close by, it permitted slavery, and it was Cuba's major trading partner. In 1842 twice as many American ships visited Havana as

Spanish; and the value of Cuban exports to the United States was double that of sales to Spain.

Restlessness among the creoles was matched by stirrings among the colored population. The intensification of sugar cultivation had worsened conditions for slaves, at least during the *zafra* or cane-cutting season in the first months of each year. While it may have been true, as often asserted, that Cuban slavery was less harsh than American because of the months of comparative idleness in sugar-producing areas and because of the protective features afforded by Catholicism and Roman law, the system was oppressive enough to cause much resentment. Abolitionism had some encouragement from Spanish sources and a great deal from British and Jamaican. Cuban slave-owners, in fact, fervently maintained that Britain wished to promote emancipation in order to ruin Cuba's competitive position in sugar. Britain pressed Spain to honor the treaty of 1817 and finally, in 1835, won permission to station a commission in Havana to free slaves imported in violation of the treaty. The traffic declined, though Spanish officials tended to wink at it for another generation. The publicity attending these developments agitated some of the colored population and promoted abolitionist sentiments. Much of it found a focus in David Turnbull, a British consul in Cuba who aspired to be a Negroes' Las Casas and was removed from his post at Spanish request. He returned in secret, however, and continued to circulate proposals for Negro freedom.

In 1843 Cuba was badly shaken by the exposure of an extensive conspiracy to raise a colored rebellion in the province of Matanzas. Turnbull was suspected, as was a prominent educator and writer, José de la Luz y Caballero, but proof was lacking. The authorities were able to implicate a mulatto poet, Gabriel de la Concepción Valdés ("Plácido") and several confederates in this so-called *Escalera* (ladder) plot and executed them. Leopoldo O'Donnell, the captain-general, suppressed the nascent insurrection with such ferocity that no further conspiracies reached the danger stage for a quarter of a century.

Fearful of losing their slaves—and paradoxically of having too many lest Cuba be Africanized—as well as dissatisfied with Spain's rule, many prominent creoles looked during the 1840s to the United

States. The acquisition of Oregon, the admission of Texas, and the conquests of the Mexican War indicated little hesitancy on the part of the northern republic to expand. Many American politicians spoke openly about taking Cuba, and President Polk made overtures to Spain to purchase the island. By the close of the decade at least three centers in Cuba functioned to promote annexation. In the capital was the Havana Club, made up of wealthy men who wanted lower land taxes and the chance to govern the island. They advanced funds to finance anti-Spanish propaganda in the United States and to raise liberating expeditions. In Puerto Príncipe there was a group of planters who operated in conjunction with a Cuban Council in New York presided over by a liberal exile named Gaspar Betancourt Cisneros. The town of Trinidad was the third and most active center.

The Trinidad group was led by General Narciso López, a Venezuelan by birth who had spent many years in the Spanish army and had been a ranking official in Cuba. Now he was a fervent Cuban patriot. Although nearly everyone who has studied his life regards him as an annexationist, a few Cuban historians believe that he favored independence. Whatever his intentions, he planned for an uprising in 1848 in which American allies would land to join the Trinidad faction. The scheme failed, and López fled to the United States. There he gathered 600 men, two-thirds of them Americans, and sailed from New Orleans, bringing into Cuba its newly devised flag with the Masonic emblem. At Cárdenas he engaged the Spanish forces with some success, but the countryside failed to rebel and he returned to the United States. In 1851 he sailed again with 500 men, only one-tenth of whom were Cubans, and planned to effect a junction with his old confederates in Trinidad. They rebelled too soon, however, and were suppressed before López could arrive to support them. Then he landed in Pinar del Río, only to find no backing whatever in that underdeveloped province. Before long the Spaniards captured and killed López and most of his men.

Hopes were not yet abandoned. Cuban exiles in the United States led by Betancourt persuaded William Quitman, a former governor of Mississippi and a general, to head another expedition. While he was assembling his forces he learned that an insurrection had been prematurely started and thwarted, in this case exposing a plan for killing the captain-general as preparation for the American landing. Deterred by this event—which involved the execution of one of the most respected leaders of the rebels, Ramón Pintó—and by further squabbling among the refugee Cuban groups, Quitman called off his invasion. Meanwhile, American sentiment for annexing or even helping Cuba was cooling. Three American diplomats had met in Ostend in 1854 to issue the Ostend Manifesto, a bombastic pronouncement that Spain must sell Cuba to the United States or have it torn from her, only to be jeered at by European governments and repudiated by their own. It was clear that American adventures in the Caribbean might be risky, and besides, the growing North-South cleavage precluded any serious schemes to add another slave state to the Union.

A firm government in Cuba during the 1850s managed to still much of the sentiment for revolution, which in no case had been overwhelming. General José de la Concha, who was captain-general for most of the decade, carried out the executions of potential rebels and tightened the administration. The office of intendant was absorbed in his own, salaried urban police provided better order, and the Volunteers, the militia composed of peninsulars and pro-Spanish Cubans, were enlarged. Concha not only flaunted the abiding military power of Spain but built roads and schools. His attention to education was overdue, since laws had called for schooling for some years, but it benefited Cuba to the extent of significantly increasing the school population to 17,000 by 1860. While Spanish administration remained slothful and corrupt, and of course in the hands of peninsulars, Concha gave it more tone. In greatly increasingly revenues, half of them derived from import duties, he demonstrated the improvements he had effected, though Cubans complained that too much of their tax money went to Spain.

An interruption of Concha's reign in 1853-55 brought General Juan M. Pezuela to the captain-general's post. A liberal and an abolitionist, Pezuela cut off the illegal slave traffic and talked of liberating unregistered slaves as well as admitting free Negroes from Jamaica. He did not remain in office long enough to carry out these policies, but they alarmed not only Cubans but some southern Americans, who constantly feared that Cuba might become a chaotic "black" nation like Haiti. As it happened, Cuba was not being Africanized as rapidly as many thought. White immigration, mostly from Spain, particularly the Canary Islands, continued to be very heavy, and the census of 1861 would show that nonwhites were still in a minority. Other racial elements were now in the picture. In 1849 the first of many contracts was let for the importation of Yucatecan Indians from Mexico, many of whom were very dark-skinned and were treated as Negro slaves. Despite occasional efforts of Mexican leaders to stop the traffic, it continued steadily for years. And Chinese contracted laborers also began to enter Cuba in considerable numbers. Whereas the Chinese tended to rise from a servile status, the Negro population remained in it with few exceptions, and white persons enforced segregation in public places as a means of stressing their claim to superiority.

During the 1860s Cuba had two sympathetic captain-generals, Francisco Serrano y Domínguez and Domingo Dulce, both of whom eased tensions between creoles and peninsulars. With annexation to the United States no longer a serious possibility, the creoles concentrated on efforts to secure reforms and autonomy within the Spanish monarchy. The Count of Pozos Dulces, one of the fifty or so Cuban noblemen, published a newspaper, *El Siglo*, which voiced the desires of the more moderate creoles, and José Antonio Saco (who had been allowed to return from exile) continued to wield much influence in behalf of liberalization under the crown. An opportunity to achieve autonomy arrived in 1865, when the Spanish overseas ministry came under control of the young scholar, Antonio Cánovas del Castillo. Impressed with the opinions of Serrano and even Concha concerning Cuban complaints, he called a *Junta de Información* of twenty-two members, half of them elected by municipal councils and half appointed from among former royal officials, to make representations for Cuba and Puerto Rico. Hopes ran high when this body met in Madrid in October 1866 for a session of six months. Saco and Pozos Dulces presented the creole program for autonomy and the promotion of commerce; the Cuban delegation disagreed about slavery but compromised in favor of gradual abolition. Dismissed with vague promises, the delegates went home, only to realize that the staggering regime of Isabel II had neither the will nor the power to reach an accommodation with the Cubans.

The Ten Years' War and the Restoration (1868-1895)

Annexation to the United States and reform within the Spanish monarchy now seemed unattainable. In Oriente province, which had undergone a spectacular growth in the past few decades, a group of creole planters turned to revolution. Their plans were advanced when an unexpected stimulus came their way in the dethronement of the incompetent and nymphomaniac Isabel II in September 1868. On October 10, at the plantation of Carlos Manuel de Céspedes near Bayamo, a group of about one hundred proclaimed rebellion. On the next day they entered the town of Yara and issued a call for independence, a republic, and the liberation of slaves who would assist the revolution. The insurrection did not seem particularly dangerous; in fact, it had been clumsily planned. Economic conditions were generally good, particularly in Havana, and the new Spanish government promised sympathetic attention to Cuban aspirations. Domingo Dulce, who returned as captain-general in January 1869, offered the islanders all of the liberties now claimed by Spaniards under the new regime, and representation in the *Cortes.* At least 20,000 Spanish regulars were stationed in Cuba, and the V*oluntarios* were soon expanded to several times that number.

Yet the revolutionists were very determined, and the mountainous character of the eastern half of Cuba made suppression difficult. Oriente fell almost entirely under their sway, and the provinces of Camagüey and Las Villas experienced some disorders during the following years. Obviously, the insurrectionists were able to maintain contact with one another in various parts of eastern Cuba, largely through the masonic brotherhood. In April 1869 a self-appointed assembly proclaimed a constitution for the republic and elected Céspedes president. Shortly thereafter, the republic asked the United States to annex it. President Grant was unwilling at this point to sponsor annexation, but he wished to grant the rebels belligerent rights until Secretary of State Fish dissuaded him. Nonetheless, in ways that are familiar in our own times, thousands of Cubans found it possible to sail to the United States or the Bahamas and to return with arms and supplies. Exiles in New York raised funds and carried out fairly effective propaganda for *Cuba libre* for some years, surviving a blast from President Grant, who denounced heroes who remained far from the scene of battle but tried to involve others in their war. On the whole, Grant's policies were legally correct, even if Cubans read sinister motives or heartlessness into them. The United States had much sympathy for the liberal experiments in Spain between 1868 and 1875 and did not make unreasonable demands that might have caused war in 1873, when the Spaniards killed a number of Americans on the crew of the "Virginius," a ship of United States registry that was illegally running guns to the Cuban rebels. This did not mean that Grant had no intention of purchasing Cuba if conditions were propitious. Spanish liberals, especially the republicans, encouraged this hope at times. But as things worked out, American purchase of Cuba was not feasible during these years, and the Grant administration, and later that of Hayes, did no more than urge the Spaniards and Cubans to reach an accommodation.

By 1870 the rebels had perhaps 40,000 men under arms. They were seldom a match for the Spaniards in pitched battles, but they were effective in cutting railroads, burning sugar mills and plantation houses, playing grim jokes on their enemies, and killing isolated loyalists. Their appeal to the Negro element diminished after the passage of a Spanish law of 1870, which freed everyone at birth and all slaves over 60, and by offers of the Spaniards to emancipate slaves who fought with them. During the early 1870s hostilities continued, usually in a desultory fashion, involving little more than terrorism by bands. The military campaigns were sufficient, however, to establish several heroes in the Cuban pantheon. Máximo Gómez, a tough warrior from the Dominican Republic who hated Spaniards, emerged as the strongest military leader. Calixto García was probably the second most important commander. Antonio Maceo, a mulatto, had the most dash and brilliance and caught the imagination of the Cubans as a folk hero. While the fighting went on, the civilian government had much difficulty maintaining its identity—it rarely had any authority—in the face of the military leaders. In October 1873, Céspedes was overthrown, to be betrayed a few months later and garroted by the Spaniards. Replacing him was Sebastián Betancourt Cisneros, a one-time marquis, who was president for a year until he was ousted at the behest of Máximo Gómez. In 1876 Tomás Estrada Palma became president but he was soon captured by the Spaniards.

At last the war wore itself out. Economic disruption reduced

Oriente and parts of Camagüey into a primitive state, and Gómez suffered a severe defeat when he attempted a major battle in 1875. Meanwhile, Spain had experienced the interim period under Serrano's regency from 1868 to 1871, the reign of the Italian Amadeo I from 1871 to 1873, and several types of republics during 1873 and 1874. Early in 1875 the son of Isabel II, Alfonso XII, returned as monarch and quickly calmed the country. The Spanish element in Cuba had maintained itself supreme throughout this period, indeed had prospered, except in the eastern areas. Royalist Cubans and peninsular Spaniards had ousted or intimidated successive captain-generals who had been conciliatory to the rebels. Yet Spanish losses were very heavy, perhaps reaching 80,000. When, in 1877, Estrada Palma was captured and 25,000 fresh Spanish troops arrived, an end to the rebellion was indicated.

Yet it required many months to liquidate the war. Marshal Arsenio Martínez Campos, who had played the crucial role in making Alfonso XII king, came to Cuba as captain-general and negotiated patiently with the rebels. In February 1878 he persuaded most of them to accept the so-called Pact of Zanjón, by which a general "forgetfulness" would cover the Ten Years' War, practically everyone would be pardoned, slaves who had fought for either side would be freed, and Cuba would take her place as an integral province of the Spanish monarchy with civil liberties and representation in the *Cortes*. Certainly the Cubans had won major concessions. With a population of 1,400,000 and an economic basis not yet dominated by any one activity, they might look forward to progress as a well-balanced society within a constitutional framework. Mocking such a prospect were bleak realities: economic ruin in Oriente, the crippling of the tobacco industry due to the transfer of much cigar-making to Florida, the virtual end of coffee production, and the need to rebuild the sugar industry in the face of competition from subsidized European sugar beet cultivation. Moreover, Spanish policies had always been characterized by fickleness and lack of understanding, or what Cubans called treachery. Ultimately, a few leaders of the recent rebellion rejected the Pact of Zanjón. Maceo and Calixto García tried to raise another insurrection in 1879-80, *la guerra chiquita* (the little war), and again in 1884 and 1885. They and others continued to brood and plot abroad. Since they considered themselves at war with Spain until

1898, patriotic Cubans often regard the struggle that began in 1868 as the Thirty Years' War.

Under Alfonso XII (1875-85) the Spanish government made some effort to reconcile the Cubans. The captain-general became a governor-general, presumably a title denoting less militarism. The army commissions that had ruled rural Cuba under virtual martial law since 1825 were abolished, and provincial deputations and municipal councils came to exercise some powers in local affairs. In 1880 the Spanish government decreed that education be compulsory and in 1886 it finally and absolutely abolished slavery, measures that gratified many segments of Cuban opinion. Yet it would not concede suffrage to creoles except those who paid twenty-five pesos a year in taxes, about 3 per cent of the population, though practically all peninsular Spaniards who held offices could vote.

The continuation of peninsular predominance in the bureaucracy and the use of nearly all Cuban revenues to support it and the military caused much dissatisfaction among the creoles. Funds were insufficient for needed public works and even for the schools that were supposed to be operating. Working through the Economic Society of Friends of the Country, the prestigious organization of wealthy planters and men of business, and a political party known as the *Autonomista*, the creoles drafted and submitted many plans for the self-government of Cuba. At times they flirted with the United States for annexation, particularly during the first Cleveland administration, and deliberately withdrew from participation in elections as a means of threatening Spain. They achieved little, and ultimately served to discredit their cause while making the programs of exiles for outright independence more attractive. In 1895 they finally wrung from Spain the so-called Abarzuza Law, which provided that the governor-general would share authority with a council of administration made up of fifteen elected and fifteen appointed members. It came too late. Rebellion had already begun. Autonomy was a lost cause, and the generally moderate and responsible *Autonomistas* would be removed from Cuban political life.

Cuba's economy after the Ten Years' War underwent a revamping that shaped the island's future for many decades. As noted, coffee cultivation and cigar-making were casualties of the rebellion. Though not extinguished, they were so reduced that many small farmers left their occupations or were absorbed in the expanding sugar industry. Conditions in the cigar-making trade were so bad that labor agitation and strikes, the first in Cuba, occurred during the last years of the century. On the other hand, the sugar industry rallied from destruction during the Ten Years' War, the depression of the 1880s, and the growth of European beet competition to become Cuba's primary economic strength. The United States market for the commodity accounted for its growth, and for the purchase by Americans of plantations. Following naturally was American involvement in the processing of sugar. Capital from the so-called Sugar Trust in the United States made it possible to establish great sugar-milling centers known as *centrales*, which had elaborate, steam-driven machinery and could process cane on a huge volume. All of this was especially important because unpropitious economic conditions called for greater efficiency if Cuban sugar was to survive foreign competition. It followed that enormous plantations or collections of properties were necessary to assure a regular flow of the cane to the crushers, and short railways into the countryside to facilitate it. Thus men with capital, often Americans, bought lands hitherto owned by *colonos* (small, independent farmers) who had carried their own cane to local mills and shared it for the expense of processing; *colonos* tended to be reduced to employees of the *centrales*. Capitalization, mechanization, and the subordination of sugar-growing to distribution pointed the way that Cuba's sugar industry was going.

American investment in the island had risen to perhaps $50,000,000 on the eve of the war with Spain. Of course, sugar was still far from monopolizing the Cuban economy, and Americans from dominating the industry. Yet the United States market was crucial to the island's prosperity. A reciprocity treaty that permitted low duties on Cuban raw sugar into the Union spelled sudden and great prosperity. When it ended with the Wilson Tariff Act of 1894, the island plunged into acute depression, a factor that made it receptive to the rebellion that began in 1895.

CUBA AS A QUASI-INDEPENDENT NATION

Cubans Destroy the Colony; Americans Oust Spain (1895-1898)

Spain had failed badly to reconcile Cuba's general desire for autonomy and its economic link with the United States to its own conceptions of loyalty. Unable to govern itself competently, the kingdom exasperated its overseas subjects in Cuba and the Philippines and failed to attach those who were fundamentally loyal. The most perceptive Spaniards knew that Cuba's moral alienation was a fact by 1895. Yet an outright grant of independence was beyond the frame of reference of the public, especially in a period when other European nations were indulging in imperialistic expansion. Sale to the United States would probably have been the most feasible course, all considered, but the political courage required for it was lacking in Madrid, attractive as the politicians might have thought the money. Without the statesmanship to rule well or to grant autonomy wholeheartedly, the Spanish government now proved itself unable to dominate the island by force.

A well-organized insurrection from the outside destroyed the colonial status of Cuba between 1895 and 1898. This was largely the work of Cuba's most admired historical figure, José Martí. Born in Havana in 1853 of Spanish parents, Martí was arrested for revolutionary activity as a teenager during the Ten Years' War and served time in a chain gang. Released and sent to Spain through the intercession of his father, a former minor official, he studied law but elected to become a writer. After a sojourn in Mexico and Guatemala, where he taught school and wrote poetry, he returned to Cuba when the Ten Years' War ended, only to be deported for subversion after a short time. The promotion of Cuban independence now became his life work. In the United States most of the time, moving among circles of Cuban exiles in Florida, New Orleans, and New York, he wrote, conspired, and agitated. Disputing and then reconciling with other exiles, a fractious group as always, he gradually acquired an ascendancy in the cause, which brought him the title of "Apostle" of *Cuba libre* by 1889. In 1892 he organized a junta in New York, brought together the scattered Cubans in other areas, and established contacts with potential insurrectionists in Cuba. He went to Haiti to tighten a rather uneasy tie with Máximo Gómez and to Costa Rica to attach Antonio Maceo. Throughout 1894 he went back and forth, from New York to Florida, to New Orleans, to Mexico, inspiring the exiles and preparing for the landings of 1895.

It is difficult to judge Martí, whose apotheosis in recent decades has placed him beyond human status. In many ways a pathetic visionary, he had an unsatisfactory marriage, suffered repeated failures in business and journalistic enterprises, and uttered so many notions that his thinking lacks consistency. Messy as his personal life was, however, he had a superb gift for propagandizing and organization. The insurrection of 1895 was deftly arranged and timed. Chaotic and colliding personalities were united, money raised, influential Americans attracted, and above all, an overpowering inspiration imparted to the cause. This inspiration was to make Cuba a free country; Martí's other ideas seem to be little more than homely maxims about virtue, duty, patriotism, and liberty. He taught Cubans to be suspicious of the United States, the monster in whose entrails, he said, he had lived. Since his death Cubans have made much of his preachments favoring civilian ascendancy over the military, anticlericalism, education, and multiracial harmony, but these had little effect on the men of 1895. Appealing as Martí must have been as an orator and writer to his contemporaries, he was something of a humorless scold. It is paradoxical that modern Cubans adore him while disregarding the puritanical aspects of his thinking.

Martí's first military effort was a fiasco. In January 1895 he planned for three ships to sail from Fernandina, Florida, to carry his own party and to fetch Gómez from Haiti and Maceo from Central America. The American authorities confiscated all three vessels, together with arms and funds. Yet he proceeded, giving the signal for an uprising in Cuba and meeting Gómez again to draft the manifesto of Montecristi(Haiti) calling for Cuban independence. The old warrior found another ship, and after a nasty quarrel over money, Maceo too agreed to join the landing. On February 24, at Baire, the war formally began. The leaders met in March in Oriente to issue the summons to rebel. Martí was greatly touched and surprised when Maceo declared him a major general. Eager to acquire military fame, Martí exposed himself to Spanish fire on May 19 at Dos Ríos and was killed. But the revolution was well under way, and it had its martyr.

The revolution readily appealed to the rural poor of Oriente and Camagüey. Martí's plans had also been soundly prepared. In September 1895, deputies chosen by the five army corps of the revolting forces met at Jimaguayu, Camagüey, to proclaim the Republic in Arms. The government was supposed to be centered in this group, the Council, with Salvador Cisneros Betancourt as its president and Bartolomé Masó as vice-president. Gómez was acclaimed *general en jefe*, with Maceo as lieutenant general. Tomás Estrada Palma was named delegate abroad to carry on diplomatic negotiations, mainly with the United States, where the New York junta was doing very effective work in propaganda and fund-raising. Actually, the Council was only a civilian front for Gómez and Maceo. Presidents Cleveland and McKinley steadily declined to recognize it as the legitimate government of Cuba despite much pressure. Meanwhile, Spanish national pride was wildly aroused. Preparations were made to reinforce indefinitely their 30,000 troops already stationed in Cuba, and the conciliatory Martínez Campos, who had pacified the island in 1878, returned as governor-general.

Neither the reputation nor the forces of Martínez Campos served to contain the new rebellion. In October 1895, Maceo and Gómez, each with scarcely more than 1,000 armed men, began a spectacular march that took them into Havana province by January 1866. Gómez declared that Cuba must be made worthless for Spain, and he ordered the end of all economic activity that benefited the royalists. His forces burned sugarcane, destroyed mills and *centrales*, and terrorized workers. Owners who declined to join his cause were stripped and often killed, and food was cut off from royalist-held towns. In a short time Cuba became a stricken island. Yet the population as a whole favored the rebellion that had so reduced it. After Maceo penetrated the western end of the island, Pinar del Río, and doubled back to meet Gómez near Havana, it was apparent that Martínez Campos' mixture of force and conciliation had failed. The soldier-statesman admitted his defeat and asked to be replaced.

During 1896 conditions worsened for both sides. Gómez and Maceo were usually able to evade the constantly growing Spanish forces and even to defeat them in occasional pitched battles. Calixto García landed in March, bringing further outside aid to the insurrectionists. Both houses of the United States Congress expressed the opinion that President Cleveland should grant belligerent rights to the Cubans, but the president refused, since American property-owners would lose their claim to indemnification from Spain and, besides, he distrusted the rebels who were reducing the island to such anarchy and poverty. On the royalist side, a turning point came with the arrival of General Valeriano Weyler, a self-proclaimed tough man of German ancestry who personified Spain's determination to hold Cuba. Weyler improved and increased the number of *trochas*, the no-man's land of trenches, blockhouses, and barbed wire that divided the island in several places. He also instituted a policy of "reconcen-tration," by which the rural population was to be removed to gar-risoned towns. Spanish forces would raid the countryside thus cleared and regard anyone they found there as rebels. This policy, which anticipated French measures in Algeria and American in Southeast Asia in the mid-twentieth century, complemented Gómez' strategy of ruin. Cuba turned into a hellish place where soldiers stalked the rural areas, killing right and left, while civilians huddled in towns where disease and food shortage took a hideous toll. American newspapers, especially the "yellow press" that used sensation to entice readers, and which in any case depended largely on the Cuban junta in New York for information, were soon identifying "Butcher" Weyler and the Spaniards as monsters.

For a time Weyler's policies seemed to promise success. Gómez was isolated in Camagüey and Oriente, and Maceo was killed after he left his base in Pinar del Río. Something of a normal life returned to Havana, where business resumed and sugar exports were still substan-tial. But American emotions were aroused, and even in Spain, the cost and terror of the war caused misgivings. William McKinley, president after March 1897, withstood congressional and public pressure to intervene in behalf of the Cuban rebels, but he warned Spain to end the reconcentration policy. And he approved secret efforts to persuade the queen-regent to sell Cuba, either to the United States or to a bizarre group of promoters who sought to purchase its independence with American backing. In October 1897 the liberal prime minister Práxedes Sagasta recalled Weyler and sent Ramón Blanco as gov-ernor-general to conciliate the Cubans.

Blanco proclaimed the end of reconcentration, though it was not effected immediately, and on January 1, 1898, implanted the autonomy plan that had been approved in 1895. But Cuba was not destined to become a self-governing province in the Spanish monarchy. The population as a whole was alienated, and the leaders had fought too long and too hard for full independence to compromise. Peninsular and royalist extremists were also adamant. Furious riots in Havana in January 1898 showed how intractable they were. The American consul asked for a warship to anchor in Havana harbor as a protection for American citizens. The battleship "Maine" arrived, and a Spanish vessel was scheduled to visit New York as a return "courtesy." On February 9, American opinion was further inflamed when Cubans published a personal letter by the Spanish minister to Washington which referred insultingly to President McKinley. On the night of February 15, the "Maine" exploded and sank, killing 266 Americans.

From this point the emotions of the American public and Congress determined the course of events. An American investigation concluded that the "Maine" had been blown up by an external agent, that the ship's ribs were bent inward. A Spanish commission arrived at the opposite conclusion. Pushed by popular anger, McKinley demanded that Spain prepare to meet the wishes of the Cuban insurgents at once. The Spanish were willing to do so, but other European governments, fearful for the safety of the Spanish throne, encouraged them to save face. Hence Spain's reply made nearly every concession that McKinley had required, but in form it constituted a technical refusal of his ultimatum. In any event, the Cubans would not negotiate at all, and McKinley was correct in minimizing the Spanish counter-proposals when, on April 11, he asked Congress to authorize him to use force to terminate Spanish rule in Cuba.

During the debates that followed the president's request, the Senate passed a resolution calling for the recognition of the Cuban republic, but the House of Representatives declined to support it, under presidential pressure. McKinley was not alone in refusing to regard the Republic in Arms as a true government. Gómez and García by now had nothing but scorn for it, and they disregarded it contemptuously. Modern Cubans, however, have deplored McKinley's stand. The president accepted the Teller Amendment, which stipulated that "the United States hereby disclaims any disposition or intention to exercise sovereignty, jurisdiction, or control over said island except for the pacification thereof, and asserts its determination when that is accomplished to leave the government and control of the island to its people." War between the United States and Spain was formally a fact by April 25.

The American regular army consisted of only 25,000 men. Spain had 190,000 regulars in Cuba alone, in addition to 70,000 *Voluntarios* and other militia. Cuban forces may have numbered 50,000, but many were ill-armed. The insurrectionists had already deprived Spain of power over most of the island but had little prospect of ever removing her armed forces from key points. This was the mission of the United States. Snubbed as it was, the Republic in Arms nonetheless placed its men under American control, and the famous "message to Garcia" established contact between Washington and General Calixto García, who commanded the strongest force of Cubans. Meanwhile, Havana had been blockaded and, after Admiral Pascual Cervera sailed his pitiful little Spanish fleet into Santiago de Cuba, so was that harbor. These naval movements practically determined the strategic pattern of "the splendid little war." A decisive land action was now necessary to compel Spain to accept the inevitable. This was forecast with the disembarkation of 17,000 American troops east of Santiago de Cuba, at Siboney and Daiquirí, in the third week of June. An advance toward the fortified places east of the city and the costly American assaults on El Caney and San Juan Hill on July 1 constituted the land campaign of the war. On July 3 the Spanish fleet was destroyed when it tried to escape from Santiago de Cuba, and on July 17 the city formally surrendered. Spanish disasters in the Pacific and an almost unopposed conquest of Puerto Rico spelled the end of an overseas empire in existence since 1493. On August 12 hostilities ceased as Spain agreed to relinquish sovereignty over Cuba.

Unfortunately, incidents during the brief Cuban campaign had large consequences on Cuban-American relations, particularly when inflated by mid-twentieth-century writers. García had advised the Americans about the best landing sites and covered the disembarkations. Cubans had supplied information about the Spanish defenses and had pinned down Spanish forces. Yet they had interpreted American orders so narrowly that they calmly sat by while the Americans engaged in fierce fighting during the battle of San Juan Hill. Also, they had failed to do more than merely harass a Spanish force of

3,000 that entered Santiago de Cuba at a critical point. American soldiers were wrathful. Already they, together with the numerous newspaper correspondents and "excursionists," had developed a lively contempt for the Cuban people, whom they saw as a mixed-blooded rabble interested more in stealing food and supplies than in fighting or working. Having glamorized the Cuban patriots so much, newspapers now vented their scorn for an ignorant, impoverished population who scarcely seemed to deserve such concern. At the surrender ceremonies in Santiago de Cuba, General William R. Shafter cruelly snubbed García and refused to allow him to participate. Later, Gómez and General Leonard Wood exchanged threats and grievances. Americans who might have thought of annexing Cuba now chilled at the idea. Cubans saw arrogance in the Yankee, and disregard for their suffering and genuine contributions to the victory.

Cuba in American Power (1898-1902)

Had Cuba exchanged one master for another? As the Spanish prepared to leave, looting shamefully on the way, American troops poured in until there were 45,000, many of whom swaggered and misbehaved. There was no sign that the Republic in Arms would be recognized. An American military government was proclaimed, with General John R. Brooke as commander. On January 1, 1899, he formally took over in Havana from the retiring Spanish governor-general. The occasion was American; Cubans were denied the long-anticipated satisfaction of parading their troops through the capital. A few weeks later, Cuban dignitaries walked away from the burial services for General Calixto García because they thought the Americans were snubbing them. Everywhere, Cuban patriots complained of American high-handedness. Americans grumbled over lack of gratitude on the part of the islanders. In truth, the United States did not know—and has never known—what to do with Cuba. Annexationist sentiment all but dissipated once the nature of the Cuban population was known at first hand. The Negroid character of a third of it aroused racism; ancient disdain for Latin American ineptitude flared; and the Cubans were indeed in a pitiful condition, many of them ragged, half-starved, and diseased. It was unthinkable to most Americans that they could join the Union in their present state. Yet they seemed far from ready to govern themselves. President McKinley elected to put things in order on the island before making final decisions, a policy that had the overwhelming support of his countrymen.

Somehow, the subtle balances by which a society operates began to function to good effect. After receiving food and medicine from the Red Cross and American army sources, most Cuban soldiers found their way home and began to raise enough crops to feed themselves. All but a few eschewed a life of crime, despite the alarming fact that they had many rifles, and went back to civilian pursuits. Order of a sort prevailed by the end of 1898. After all, no one was more eager for peace than the Cubans.

General Brooke's government consisted of a cabinet with four Cuban ministers who, under his direction, operated the remnants of the existing bureaucracy. Police and rural guards were restored. Each province had a Cuban governor and an American general at its head, with the latter exercising real control. Most of the 138 municipal governments were restored. Americans took over the customs, which was the principal source of revenue, the postal service (where the only scandal occurred), and sanitation and health agencies. In the most disorganized areas, such as Oriente, exceptional measures were required to restore civilized life. The American ruler of that province, General Leonard Wood, took harsh but salutary steps to this end. So great was his success—and so strong were his connections in Washington—that he began to intrigue for Brooke's position. Other army officials performed well. Considering the limited experience of the army, or indeed of the United States, in such activities, the new system was installed with dispatch and good results.

Disarming the Cuban forces proved a painful problem. As long as the Cuban leaders were estranged from the Americans there remained a danger that another rebellion would break out, as soon happened in the Philippines. Gómez and other commanders thought that the Americans should pay the Cuban forces for their services since 1895, and at a much higher rate than American soldiers received. This sum, together with fantastic compensation to the higher-ranking officers, might have reached $60,000,000. The United States refused, offering no more than $3,000,000, enough to give each soldier who turned in his rifle $75. For some time the matter caused much rancor. When Gómez finally accepted the American proposal, the Cuban "government" deposed him; but when opinion rallied to his side, the Republic in Arms dissolved itself. After a tense period, Cuban soldiers began to appear to surrender their arms and take their money. The danger of insurrection vanished, and American forces were reduced to 11,000 men, a third of the size of Spain's regular army in Cuba in 1895.

Constructive measures taken by the military government gave the occupation a good reputation both in the United States and Cuba. Most of them were begun by Brooke, but in December 1899 he was replaced by General Leonard Wood. A dynamo of a man who labored at high pressure and drove his subordinates, Wood carried through the most admired achievements of the reconstruction. A census was completed in 1900, one which underlined the backward educational and economic status of the 1,500,000 Cubans, whose population had declined by 200,000 since 1895. Schooling was an urgent problem. More than 3,000 public schools were set up and 265,000 pupils enrolled. Through private gifts, nearly 1,500 Cuban teachers spent the summer of 1900 at Harvard University receiving specialized instruction. The University of Havana was restaffed and reequipped, and private schools were aided. It is true that enthusiasm for education soon slackened and that enrollments fell sharply, but a beginning had been made. At first the Americans hoped to implant Anglo-Saxon procedures in the judicial system, but soon they contented themselves with continuing the prevailing ones, establishing a supreme tribunal and other courts, and encouraging honesty by paying salaries to judges and other court officers. An American effort to breathe life into the municipal governments, long moribund under Spanish rule, made little progress against the entrenched tradition of centralization.

Church-state relations posed a delicate situation, which was handled with tact. Anticlericalism among the revolutionary leaders and the languid nature of Cuban Catholicism, as well as the emigration of many Spanish priests, made it unlikely that Cuba would be a clerical state. But the Church had rights to property and cemeteries which the Americans decided to honor, and Wood wisely agreed that civil and church marriages would be equally respected. Public works brought relief to many unemployed Cubans and effected permanent improvements in the way of roads, bridges, and sanitation facilities. Railroads, which consisted of short lines in the west and numerous private lines on sugar properties, were restored. Though the Foraker

Act forbade the issuance of franchises to United States citizens during the occupation, ways were found to circumvent it and to begin the building of a railroad from Santiago de Cuba to the Havana area with the equivalent of a franchise. Eradication of mosquitoes was the most celebrated achievement of the occupation. An American officer, Dr. Walter Reed, verified the theory previously advanced by the Cuban, Dr. Carlos Finlay, that mosquitoes were the carriers of yellow fever and malaria. An imaginative campaign soon destroyed most of the insects and made Cuba the healthiest of all tropical lands.

While the occupation was proving a gratifying success, Washington was haunted by the problem of Cuba's future relationship with the United States. It was known that significant elements in the island favored annexation to the United States—the conservative and Spanish classes and, surprisingly, a few elderly but famous revolutionary leaders. Among the Americans, annexationist sentiment was spotty. General Wood himself at one time favored Americanizing the island as preparation for eventual absorption in the Union, but he and others of this view lost their enthusiasm as they realized the gaping differences between Cubans and Americans. A perpetual occupation was contrary to American traditions. Yet Washington was aware of the business opportunities that a dependent Cuba might offer. Humanitarianism and good sense alike argued against letting the Cubans have complete freedom to turn their island into a Haiti, as so many phrased it. And then, as always, strategic considerations demanded a special status for Cuba, for the United States now regarded itself as a great power and was suspicious of European designs on the Caribbean. It had plans for a large navy and a canal across Central America. Altruistic, strategic, and selfish motives, as well as the vagaries of political pressures in American political life, called for a solution by which Cuba might constitute a source of strength to the United States and yet govern itself.

Preparing the Cubans to take over their own destiny involved deciding which of them should vote, a matter that had caused much friction in Spanish days. An electoral law issued in April 1900 granted Cuban suffrage to adult males who elected Cuban citizenship (the right of opting to be Spanish subjects had been available) and who were literate, or had served in the army, or owned $250 worth of property. In June, in the first elections, which were to fill municipal offices, the revolutionary groups won most of the seats. Then a constituent convention was called, partly to still criticism in the United States as the elections of 1900 approached. Thirty-one delegates were chosen by the 30 per cent of the Cuban electorate who bothered to vote. Again, advanced elements won, to the uneasiness of the occupying authorities. The convention met, and General Wood refrained from interfering as it prepared a constitution which provided for universal suffrage, a popularly elected president, a senate and a chamber of deputies, and separation of Church and state.

By the time the Cuban constitution was completed, early in 1901, the Americans had defined their position for the future relationship of the two countries. Mainly the work of Secretary of War Elihu Root, the conditions were: Cuba should make no treaty that would impair her sovereignty; she should contract no foreign debt whose interest could not be paid through ordinary revenues after defraying the current expenses of government; the United States might intervene for the preservation of Cuban independence or the maintenance of a government adequate for the protection of life, liberty, and property; all acts of the United States during the occupation would be validated; Cuba would execute plans for sanitation; the Isle of Pines should be omitted from the proposed boundaries of Cuba; and the United States might purchase or lease lands necessary for coaling or naval stations. These points were subsequently incorporated into a rider to an army appropriations act of 1901 and are known as the Platt Amendment.

General Wood presented the terms to a commission of the constituent convention during the course of a railway trip. The reaction was highly unfavorable, particularly over the clauses regarding debt, intervention, and naval bases. The Cubans also wished to include assurances that their sugar—production of which was just recovering from the war—could be admitted to the United States at a low tariff rate. Opposition flared in the convention itself and in the Cuban press, as well as in some circles, mainly Democratic, in the United States. The Americans did not budge at all. It was clear that Cuba must swallow the Platt Amendment, even incorporate it into the new constitution as an appendix, or else have the occupation continue indefinitely. Perhaps the terms represented a true compromise of the least the Americans would accept and the most the Cubans could give, but it had not been negotiated. Cuba, of course, had to accept it. On June 12, by a divided vote, the convention bowed. The so-called Permanent Treaty of 1903 further formalized the relations of the two countries. A reciprocal tariff act of that year gave Cuban products a reduction of 20 per cent of the usual rate for import duties into the United States and gave selected American products prefer-ence in Cuban rates.

For nearly a year after the ratification of the Platt Amendment the Americans remained in Cuba, completing their program for stabiliz-ing the island politically and witnessing the first elections for repub-lican rule. General Máximo Gómez was expected to be the first president, but the old Dominican-born warrior refused because of his advanced age and his contention that soldiers were not good men of peace. He made public criticisms of the United States, but it is pos-sible that he really favored eventual annexation. Bartolomé Masó, a recent president of the defunct Republic in Arms, ran for president as a strident critic of the Platt Amendment. Tomás Estrada Palma—president during the last stages of the Ten Years' War, delegate abroad during the recent war, and a long-time resident of the United States—secured the support of Gómez and most of the other revolu-tionaries. Estrada Palma was skeptical of Cuba's future as an inde-pendent nation, and he too apparently favored eventual annexation. Since it seemed obvious that Estrada Palma was going to win, most of Masó's supporters boycotted the polls and thus made Estrada Palma's victory overwhelming. On May 20, 1902, General Wood formally proclaimed the end of the occupation, and the Stars and Stripes came down. Cuban sovereignty became a fact as Tomás Estrada Palma entered upon his duties. A cordial mood prevailed. The numerous festivities included both official and popular expressions of gratitude to General Leonard Wood.

Faltering Steps of the New Republic (1902-1909)

Cuba entered on her republican career with advantages that made it seem likely she would escape the dreary disorders that had marred the history of other Latin American nations. She occupied an entire island and had no neighbors to dispute her boundaries. The Americans had every intention of seeing the new country succeed but hoped to leave it alone. They had set things in order, planned to purchase its chief exports, and would see that foreign powers did not molest it. Militarism, clericalism, racial tensions, urban-rural hatreds, latifundia, and caste systems—all of the familiar causes of instability in Latin America—were weak or lacking. The new government was popularly elected and headed by a beloved, capable president. If standards of living and health were low, they were the best in the West Indies, and the revolution of rising expectations had not yet made the masses restless. And yet, the Cuban republic was destined to falter from the first and has never lived up to its promise.

Tomás Estrada Palma was almost 67 when he took office. A man of great modesty, he was known to be altruistic and strictly honest. Despite his long residence abroad—or because of it—he discerned the real weakness of his compatriots. Cuba, he often said, had become a republic, but it lacked citizens. Certainly the people were nationalistic enough, as they had demonstrated in the independence struggle. Yet they had a tradition of nearly four centuries under Spain which caused them to regard the government as something to defy or exploit. Cynicism was a common attitude, as was fault-finding. Cubans had never cherished political virtue in the sense of observing integrity themselves and demanding it of others, of sacrificing for the state in undramatic workaday ways for long periods. Generations of pirates, smugglers, slave-dealers, and thieving public officials had set evil examples. Killing, rapine, and robbery in the independence struggles had undermined the decencies which spell civilization. Estrada Palma well knew this, and former schoolmaster of many years' experience in New York State that he was, he lectured to his people about their collective character defects. The Cubans liked this, as they also appreciated the scoldings that the late José Martí had written and those of a new spokesman for their conscience, Enrique José Varona. Cubans, as Fidel Castro would one day show, applaud puritanical preachments which they have no intention of heeding.

There were, of course, more mundane reasons for Cuba's failure to become a model republican democracy. The tropical climate induced languor and indolence. There was a great deal of unemployment because of the economic situation, and the nature of sugarcane raising was such that workers were idle at least half the year. The island had not really recovered from the recent war. Sugar prices were low and other products brought little money from abroad. Unhappily, the classes that had the most money and education held themselves aloof from politics. Many of them favored annexation to the United States and were scornful of local politicians who were likely to be their social inferiors. Others had been tarnished with pro-Spanish or *Autonomista* sentiments in recent years and could not be elected to any office. Except for Estrada Palma and a very small group, most of the new officeholders were grasping, vulgar, ill-educated, and eager to make up for lost time.

To Estrada Palma it seemed obvious that Cuba should advance by exporting her products, encouraging foreign investment, and stimulating white immigration while continuing the educational and public works projects of the occupation. In these policies he was very successful. He pressed the United States to agree to a reciprocity treaty, which President Theodore Roosevelt had much difficulty in getting through the Senate, owing to sugar interests which were reluctant to increase competition. As noted, the treaty was ratified in 1903. By 1904 Cuba was producing as much sugar as she had in 1894, more than one million tons, and the industry was spreading rapidly into the backward provinces of Camagüey and Oriente. Estrada Palma also scored when he persuaded the Americans to lease instead of purchase the naval stations, and to be satisfied with two, Guantánamo and Bahía Hondo, rather than four. He also won a treaty from Roosevelt by which the United States relinquished its claim to the Isle of Pines.* Foreign capital flowed into Cuba, European more than American. The Yankee stake grew from close to $50 million in 1895 to $200 million in 1906, equally divided among sugar, tobacco, and ranching. To most Cubans of that time such development was looked upon as no evil whatever but rather as an immense benefit. Correct, even cordial, relations with Spain reassured the large Spanish element in the island, which continued to manage plantations and businesses. Immigrants from Spain arrived in the greatest numbers ever, 10,000 in 1902 and 40,000 in 1905. One-fourth of the Cuban budget was

* The Americans never made use of Bahía Hondo and returned it in 1912. Because of the intrigues of a few U.S. citizens on the Isle of Pines, the Senate did not ratify the 1903 treaty until 1925, but all along it was administered as part of Cuba.

devoted to education, and public works were constructed on a scale three times that of the occupation. And the president handled finances so prudently that taxes were low and surpluses piled up in the treasury.

In spite of these accomplishments there was a disturbing undercurrent. Corruption at all levels revealed itself. Appropriations were misspent, accounts padded, and too many officeholders performed no services. The Cuban congress wanted to install the lottery again; Estrada Palma vetoed it. The congress then pressured him into borrowing $35 million abroad to pay bonuses to the warriors of liberation. Yet politicians at the higher levels and fraudulent claimants at the lower caused much of the money to be misdirected. Many were unhappy because the president refused to allow Cuba to have an army of more than a few hundred men, plus 3,000 rural guards. Cuban congressmen were persistent in thinking up proposals to spend the budget surplus, and aggrieved because Estrada Palma blocked them. When he called upon them to pass organic laws to replace the Spanish codes and the occupation regulations, they dawdled and so often refused to show up for quorum calls that weeks went by without any congressional activity.

Perhaps the real reason for the unedifying behavior of the politicians was the impending election of December 1905. Two parties had shaped up: the Conservative Republicans and the National Liberals. Personalism rather than issues divided them, though the latter party was more outspoken about the iniquities of the Platt Amendment. Estrada Palma had sought to remain above the factions, but early in 1905 he identified himself with the Conservative Republicans, who changed their name to Moderates, and announced that he would seek reelection. In March he installed a "cabinet of combat," which proceeded to remove officeholders unfriendly to the Moderates and to pad the vote registers. In reply, the Liberals boycotted the congress completely, made extravagant accusations against the administration, and plotted uprisings. A poor precedent indeed was being set for the first unsupervised presidential election. The Liberal candidate for president was José Miguel Gómez, governor of Santa Clara, with Alfredo Zayas as vice-presidential nominee. Having done as much as the administration, or more, to debase the campaign, they finally instructed their followers not to vote because the election would be rigged. Accordingly, the Moderates won everything. Estrada Palma was reelected president, his reputation considerably tarnished.

A sputtering of revolts occurred during the following months, but the administration suppressed them by arresting as many Liberals as it could catch. The United States refrained from interfering, even with advice, and had no suspicion that Cuba might explode. Both Washington and Havana were greatly surprised in August 1906 when a massive Liberal uprising occurred in Pinar del Río, to spread quickly over the rest of the island. The ranking official at the American legation was a secretary of little experience, who asked President Roosevelt for warships and marines. The president was shocked, for he had no intention of intervening. At the very moment of this crisis his secretary of state, Elihu Root, was touring South America seeking to allay fears of Yankee imperialism. Roosevelt asked the consul-general in Havana, a former soldier of the occupation who had become a businessman, Frank M. Steinhardt, to take over the legation. Steinhardt too thought the situation perilous in the extreme. On September 8 he transmitted to Roosevelt an appeal from President Estrada Palma to intervene. Yet Roosevelt refused, though he sent warships to the waters near Havana and asked Secretary of War William Howard Taft to go to that city.

Taft arrived on September 19, to find the government at bay, with only a few hundred troops and the 3,000 rural guards scattered about the island to listen to its orders. He busily interviewed many Cubans and negotiated with administration and Liberal leaders. Taft concluded that the recent elections had been fraudulent and that a majority favored the Liberals. Yet he opposed backing down before insurrectionists. The plan he devised was to nullify all of the elections but those of the president and vice-president and to hold fresh ones. The Liberals accepted this proposal and agreed to lay down their arms. Taft was dismayed when President Estrada Palma refused it, on the grounds that the honor and dignity of his office, and himself, could not admit that the elections were dishonest, and that "criminals" must not be rewarded for rebelling. It may have been that Taft had not treated the old gentleman tactfully. In later years the United States would generally support an administration in power, regardless of the legitimacy of its origin. On this occasion it was sponsoring a compromise which really insulted the president. In any event, Estrada Palma and the vice-president resigned, and the Moderates refused to attend congress.

The government of Cuba had disappeared. Taft then ordered the landing of 2,000 marines and shortly after, 5,600 American troops. It was not difficult to dissuade the Liberals from fighting, for they had unseated Estrada Palma. Soon most of them were disarmed peacefully. A provisional government was proclaimed by Taft on September 29. The Cuban flag would still fly, and the Cuban administration function. The situation would last, he promised, only long enough to restore order and hold elections. In Cuba the reaction was largely favorable. Both the Liberals and the fallen administration had hoped for intervention. The lesson seemed to be that a party that lost an election could bring about American interference to defeat its opponents.

Estrada Palma quietly disappeared into the country, eventually to his modest holdings in Bayamo, where he died in poverty in 1907. Taft ruled as acting governor until October 13, 1906, when Charles E. Magoon took over. A lawyer from Nebraska who had been governor of the Panama Canal Zone, Magoon was a large, amiable man who had many virtues but who lacked the flair of dramatizing his achievements. Reasonably popular during his stay in Havana, he afterward became the target of fantastic charges of personal and official dishonesty. He remained longer than expected; not until December 1908 were the politicians ready to hold elections, and the occupation lasted until January 1909. Magoon's accomplishments were substantial. Under his sponsorship organic laws covering the functioning of the local governments, electoral bodies, judiciary, and civil service were drawn up. A Cuban-American commission that he appointed, headed by Colonel Enoch H. Crowder, prepared these codes and revised them in the light of public criticism. Public works continued on a very large scale, though Cuba still lagged in railroads, highways, and docks after these efforts. A census taken in 1907 revealed a sharp population growth, reversing the stagnation or decline since 1868. Now there were two million Cubans.

The criticisms of Magoon center partly on the fact that he inherited a treasury surplus of $13 million and left one of only $3 million. The charge is misleading, for the Cuban congress had previously made extensive appropriations that ate into Estrada Palma's savings, and the revolution of 1906 had been costly. Furthermore, a hurricane and a yellow fever epidemic caused unusual disbursements, while the panic of 1907 reduced revenues. Accusations that Magoon condoned graft had some basis, though he did not enrich himself. A cherished Cuban belief that he invented the system of *botella*, or padded political jobs, is based on the false notion that the previous Spanish and Cuban administrations had not made this discovery for themselves. Yet it may have been that the American governor was overly eager to placate the Liberals in the interest of harmony and that he awarded them too many political plums, contracts, and pardons. In any event, most Cubans have long been taught that Magoon instituted a system of graft.

Thanks to the American presence, the elections of 1908 went off properly. The Liberals split between the Gómez and Zayas factions —a rivalry that would plague Cuban politics for many years—but finally nominated Gómez for president and Zayas for vice-president. The Conservatives (previously the Moderates) chose General Mario García Menocal. In the December election the Liberals won by 201,000 to 130,000 and carried all twenty-four seats in the senate. More than two-thirds of the electorate went to the polls, and peace prevailed. When the occupation ended, on January 28, 1909, many Cubans publicly praised Charles Magoon for his recent services.

Tawdry Political Life and Economic Boom (1909-1925)

José Miguel Gómez was probably as popular a president as Cuba has ever had. Fifty-one when he took office, he had a distinguished record in the independence struggle, when he had been a major general. Afterward, he was an appointed governor under the American occupation for his native province of Santa Clara (also known as Las Villas) and had been elected governor under the republic. A true caudillo of the usual Latin American pattern in a province that boasts an individuality that sets it apart from the others, Gómez was a charismatic hero to the populace and a genial tyrant. His admirers saw him as a true man of the people, a democrat who loved liberty and tolerance. To his enemies he was a crafty manipulator of personalities, who could ruin, even murder, his opponents and whose driving force was greed. Nearly everyone agreed that he was immensely attractive as a person, that he was truly *simpático*.

The four years of his term, from 1909 to 1913, were generally sunny times, with sugar harvests growing steadily and small industries developing along with the spread of automobiles, electricity, and other features of modern life. American investments expanded little, due to the depression following the panic of 1907, and Europeans owned more of Cuba than did Americans. Yet business was usually good. Gómez regarded himself as its friend, a quite respectable attitude at this period for a political figure. He also made gestures unusual for the times in favor of urban labor, such as advocating a university for workers and fostering low-cost housing. He benefited rural workers with a law that required employers to pay them in cash rather than chits to be redeemed at company stores. A seemingly amiable figure who favored everybody, Gómez—and most of his contemporaries in public life—had only a dim awareness of the dangerous social problems that were developing.

Gómez' admirers call his administration "fecund" in all branches of national affairs. Cuba established relations with nearly every other nation and built up a showy diplomatic corps. Gómez created an army of several thousand to keep his enemies from doing to him what he had done to Estrada Palma, and he started a small navy and coast guard. Some of the organic laws and codes begun under Magoon were completed. Education received much praise and some financing. A few agricultural schools were opened, the national museum established, and academies of arts, letters, and history organized. With mixed motives, Gómez greatly stimulated the construction of railways, dredging of ports, draining of swamps, and beautification of Havana. In restoring cock-fighting and the lottery, so beloved in Spanish times, he was doing what appealed to most Cubans, dubious as the social effects may have been.

Yet the critics of Gómez have a strong case. He shamelessly enriched himself and allowed members of his official family to make fortunes in government service. The traditional corruption, which had been interrupted only during the Brooke-Wood regime, showed up at all levels unrebuked. Gómez' budgets were three times as large as those of Estrada Palma and the bureaucracy was expanded and debauched to a shocking degree. He was inhibited by few restraints in bribing or forcing congressmen, local rulers, and judges to debase the constitutional system. Conservative charges that he employed drastic means, even assassination, to have his way probably had some basis.

Several incidents tested Cuban-American relations during the Gómez years. To be sure, the nature of these relations changed after Taft became president in 1909 with Philander C. Knox as his secretary of state. While neither wished to annex Cuba, or to intervene, both were mindful of the consequences of American inattention during Estrada Palma's administration and anxious to prevent dangerous situations from arising again. As they realized the improvident and reckless nature of some of Gómez' policies, they unashamedly brought pressure to curb them. In January 1911, for example, nearly every important politician joined a company to dredge Cuban ports, an obvious need. It was planned to borrow money abroad for this purpose and to pay it back by raising import duties for the next thirty years, with the company retaining the difference between the increased revenues and the cost of retiring the debt—a difference that would be several times the outlay. Washington found ways to discourage English bankers who were on the point of advancing the funds and to secure major changes in the arrangement.

Another incident could have led to civil war. An organization of war veterans became extremely aggressive, demanding the dismissal of all officeholders who had royalist connections in the recent insurrection. When Gómez showed signs of submitting to this pressure, which might have been followed by others, Washington advised him to stand firm. He did so, probably glad to have this support, but to many Cubans it appeared that the United States was meddling in internal affairs. In another incident, the Zapata Swamp concession, Washington believed that "a barefaced steal" was in the making to enrich Gómez and his associates through a draining project. After pointedly advising the Cubans that wrongs of this type might have to be righted under a future American occupation, the Taft administration came to be persuaded that its fears were unfounded and withdrew objections.

A more dangerous affair arose in 1912, when a Negro party led by Evaristo Estenoz and Pedro Ivonet charged that Negroes, whom they claimed had done most of the fighting in the wars for independence, were being denied their share of political jobs. Since the Negro vote was essential to the Liberals, Gómez was fearful of its defection and had congress pass a law forbidding the organization of political parties on the basis of race, whereupon Estenoz and Ivonet rebelled. The Negroes appealed to President Taft to intervene. When he declined, they set about destroying foreign-owned property in the hope of forcing American landings. Taft sent reinforcements to Guantánamo and ships to hover around Cuban ports. In May, when the rebellion spread, he ordered a few marines to Daiquirí to protect foreign property but informed Gómez that this did not constitute intervention. Gómez retorted that indeed it did. It soon developed that the rebellion was not as serious as had been indicated, and Cuban forces repressed it.

Gómez had stood his ground with the United States without being provocative. Strongly as some elements of the Cuban press and political world had objected to Yankee warnings, the president may have sensed that serious dangers might have arisen had Uncle Sam been more careless. The stand of Gómez did not help him politically. In 1908, when the Gómez and Zayas factions of the Liberals effected a nervous alliance, Gómez had promised that he would not run for reelection and that Zayas could have the Liberal nomination. Since then friction between the two men had been sharp, and there was much reason to suppose that Gómez would have liked the nomination himself. But Zayas was too skillful to let the president cheat him of it, and Gómez was decent, or prudent, enough not to use force to gain it. Hence Zayas ran as the Liberal candidate with the nominal support of Gómez. The Conservatives named Mario García Menocal and the eminent writer, Enrique José Varona, as their respective presidential and vice-presidential candidates. The vote was close, 215,000 for Menocal and 201,000 for Zayas, with the Conservatives winning control of congress. It was an open secret that President Gómez had undermined Zayas and facilitated Menocal's victory. More would be heard of the feud of the two Liberals.

There was every reason to suppose that Mario García Menocal would prove a good president. A genuine hero of the wars of independence, in which he had been chief of staff for Calixto García and had won the battle of Las Tunas, Menocal (he preferred to use his mother's family name) had spent most of his youth in the United States. He graduated from Cornell University and worked for an American firm in Nicaragua as an engineer. After independence he was chief of the Havana police for a time and the operator of perhaps the largest sugar plantation of its type. Fine looking, well-educated, successful, a gentleman who mixed comfortably with the working classes, he appeared to have every asset for leadership.

Times were not of the best when Menocal took office in 1913. Sugar crops were unusually poor during his first two years, and tobacco production was low. For more than a year after World War I began Cuba suffered from loss of markets and access to European capital. American investments were only $265 million, little more than they had been a decade before, and they were not expanding fast. Labor troubles in a few of the new small industries threatened. And the inflated and demoralized bureaucracy inherited from Gómez, even though it had been largely restaffed by Conservatives, was more of a drag than an instrument for progress.

For about half his first term, Menocal seemed to be striving competently to improve conditions. Education, public health, agricultural and pastoral modernization, and labor conditions received attention. A compulsory compensation law for workingmen was enacted. Menocal virtuously but vainly sought to end the lottery, which had become a debauching influence, and he vetoed bills to permit gambling at the race tracks and jai alai courts. He exposed the corruption of the previous administration and even threatened former President Gómez with prosecution, despite the decisive role Gómez had played in making Menocal president. Menocal pleased Washington by ending the concession for port-dredging, but only the work was interrupted, not the increased revenues which were to finance it. The United States smiled on him as he negotiated a loan from the Morgan interests, for he seemed to be setting things in order. Menocal gave Cuba its own currency, to replace the Spanish, American, and French monies that had been used, a currency based on that of the United States with exactly the same denominations. And times improved by 1915, when the sugar harvest reached the new record of 3,000,000 tons.

And yet Menocal would join the long list of Cuban rulers who disenchanted their well-wishers. His administration soon became as corrupt and ineffective as that of Gómez, or more so. Enormous fortunes were made by the president's relatives and official family. Suspicions about his own integrity were widespread. It became clear that agreeable plans for progress that had been enunciated with fanfare somehow failed to materialize. Menocal even lost control of congress and almost of his own party. A painful indication of his loss of moral authority was the defection of his vice-president, the respected mentor Enrique José Varona.

Menocal had promised that he would not stand for reelection. As prosperity came, however, and with it a gratifying increase in treasury receipts, he changed his views. After much behind-the-scene negotiation, he won the nomination of his own party, the Conservatives. Opposing him were the Liberals, who had again united after a period of splinterization. Those inveterate rivals, former President Gómez and Dr. Alfredo Zayas, composed their differences sufficiently for Zayas to receive the nomination. The Liberals made it clear that they intended to win. They were surely the majority party, and they had a good case against Menocal. The Woodrow Wilson administration favored Menocal, but the United States had no inclination to intervene in the election. During the months before the election of November 1, 1916, the Cuban electorate seemed bent on proving its unwillingness to operate a true republican system. Shootings, beatings, and intimidation of all sorts gave the island an atmosphere of impending civil war. The Conservative administration resorted to harsh repressive measures, justifying them with the score of forty-two killings their partisans had suffered to seven for the Liberals. Military commissions under orders from Havana forcibly superseded many local electoral authorities on the eve of the test. Voting registers were padded in favor of the side that had the most force in any given locality.

On election night it seemed certain that Zayas had won. Despondency in the presidential palace, however, was lifted by mysterious decisions which led to the minister of interior illegally taking charge of the election returns sent to Havana. By his announcement, the election was very close, so much so that only an analysis of districts in Oriente and Santa Clara would show who had won. These ballots disappeared, and the Liberals cried fraud. The central electoral board and the supreme court upheld their complaints.

At this point the United States, which had just had a close election of its own and was preoccupied with World War I, directed Menocal to hold fresh elections in the disputed districts and made it clear to the Liberals that revolution would not be tolerated. The Liberals had no confidence in Menocal's ability to conduct honest elections and decided to resort to force regardless of the American warning. They recalled how they had gained their point in this fashion in 1906. And former President Gómez believed that most of the Cuban army would be loyal to him as its creator. Oddly, he was now master of the Liberals and strategist of the rebellion. Zayas, the recent nominee in whose behalf these efforts were undertaken, was either shrewd enough—or cowardly enough, as many Liberals thought —to hold himself aloof. Gómez ordered Liberals not to participate in the new elections called for February 1917. Meanwhile, he was planning an uprising of the Havana garrison and his own triumphal march from Santa Clara.

President Menocal was a good general too. He nipped the Havana revolt as soon as it began, arrested all available Liberal trouble-makers, and managed to maintain control over most of the army. While the Liberals alarmed the United States with threats to destroy foreign-owned properties and with intimations of pro-German sentiments, Menocal made it plain that he was President Wilson's friend. Hence the United States sold him rifles and ammunition and sent warships with landing forces to patrol the threatened areas. Since war with Germany was impending, Cuba must remain quiet. Islands of strategic importance could not indulge in civil war at such times. In March 1917, Menocal's forces penetrated the rebellious areas and captured Gómez. The revolution collapsed. Elections in the disputed regions favored the Conservatives, all the more so since Liberals did not vote, and Menocal was declared reelected.

Menocal tidied up the disruption caused by the rebellion and saw to it that many Liberals were sentenced to hard labor or death. Following Spanish tradition, however, he soon pardoned most of them, and no one was executed. Former President Gómez remained in jail for a few months and under house arrest longer, but he was not prosecuted. His popularity soared while that of Zayas, at least among Liberals, sank. Cubans were rapidly learning how to behave like many other Latin Americans. Elections were meant to be dishonest, administrations profitable, and revolutions part of the game. Varona and others deplored American intervention, moral or otherwise, and demanded that Cubans learn their own lessons in the art of self-government, even if the process was bloody and slow.

On April 7, 1917, just one day after the United States declared war on Germany, President Menocal took Cuba into the conflict. German property was confiscated, loans floated in the United States, and presidential wartime powers wielded with little restraint. Cuba became, in fact, something of an autocracy. Her contribution to the war effort was slight, only a few hundred doctors and nurses being sent to Europe and Cuban ships participating in naval patrols. A draft act was passed but did not become operative. The United States had reinforced Guantánamo during the recent disturbances, but it desired a more extensive deployment of its forces because of fears that the Germans might promote revolution or cane-burning. Menocal agreed to permit the U.S. Marines to land in Oriente and Camagüey, supposedly for training purposes. There were never more than 3,000 at any one time, but they remained long after the war.

Cuba's true importance in the war had to do with her sugar production. After tedious negotiations the Allies agreed to purchase her entire crop at 4.6¢ a pound. This was less than the Cubans desired or the United States originally favored, but British and French Caribbean sugar interests had to be considered. Of course, Cuba could not have sold her products to anyone else during the war and had to accept the Allied offer. The result of this arrangement was a spurt in prosperity which began the famous "Dance of the Millions." Production 1918-19 was 4,000,000 tons, compared to 1,500,000 tons ten years earlier, and sugar exports accounted for 89 per cent of Cuba's total, in contrast to only 54 per cent in 1909. Fantastic profits went to sugar-growers and processors. Workers enjoyed full employment and good wages. It was even necessary to import numerous Jamaicans and Haitians to help harvest the crops. When wartime controls were lifted early in 1919 the price of sugar shot up to 22.5¢ a pound. Land values quintupled, and banks made reckless loans to speculators who bought small farms and put them together in vast plantations. Many a *colono* was tempted to sell his land, only to lose the money in gambling or through inflation. Furthermore, a spending spree exhilarated the cities, where construction of luxury hotels, casinos, and ornate homes went on apace. The most unhappy groups were urban laborers, who suffered from high prices. A wave of strikes in the summer of 1919 illustrated this dissatisfaction, but Menocal broke them with the comforting knowledge that American warships were near Havana if he needed help.

President Menocal's reputation underwent further tarnishing as the Dance of the Millions encouraged his henchmen to ostentatious extravagance and unconcealed grafting. It became apparent that the much-praised educational system was sagging: attendance had fallen by a third, many teachers drew their salaries but performed no duties, and appropriations for school buildings disappeared. The same situation prevailed in public works, where contractors and allied politicians absorbed public funds and gave little to show for them. The lottery was abused to the point of scandal, with political favorites purchasing tickets at low rates and illegally selling them at high ones. Race-track and jai alai gambling was prevalent, despite the government's supposed disapproval. The regime had become a sorry affair.

The collapse of sugar prices in October 1920 caused such a bank panic that a moratorium had to be declared, and later renewed. By 1921 sugar would bring only 1.6¢ a pound, and bankruptcies and unemployment would be tragically pervasive. Every bank in the island except three owned by foreigners would fail. Foreclosures ruined many a speculator of the Dance of the Millions. Often their properties went to foreigners, mainly Americans, or to richer men who operated large plantations. Thus absentee ownership and concentration of property made great headway. Small farmers were further depressed and often forced into working for low wages when they could find employment at all.

There seemed scant possibility that the elections of 1920 would improve either the economic depression or the political situation. Former President Gómez, the Liberal candidate, was scarcely a reformer. Neither was his old rival, Alfredo Zayas, who now had organized a small Popular Party. President Menocal, after trying in vain to obtain United States advice for a Conservative successor, settled on the ex-Liberal Zayas, who formed a National League with Conservatives and Populars. In view of their experiences in 1916 the Liberals pressed for reforms in the electoral system, to which Menocal assented. Major General Enoch Crowder, whose exemplary work during the Magoon period was respected, prepared a new code, which the Cuban congress passed, that tightened controls over voter registration and counting of ballots. The Liberals begged the United States to supervise the elections, but Washington was unwilling to do more than issue warnings and station observers at certain polling places. As in 1916, Menocal again found ways to cheat. Violence was even more prevalent than before; the election was characterized by intimidation at voting points, snatching of ballot boxes by soldiers, and miscounting of votes by armed officials. Still, the result was close and confused by many disputed returns.

Shortly after the election, President Wilson, whose own party had suffered a devastating defeat, sent General Crowder back to Havana as his special representative, a move that insulted President Menocal and delighted the Liberals. Only a brief investigation was necessary to convince him that the elections had been fraudulent and that fresh ones should be held in many districts, a decision also reached by the Cuban supreme court. As in 1916-17, the Liberals complained that they could not win any test at the polls supervised by Menocal and they boycotted the by-elections. Therefore Zayas won them and the presidency. Twice the Liberals felt that they had been robbed of victory through the meddling of the United States.

In most of the world the 1920s was a decade in which statesmen failed to define and deal with major problems and thus suffered terrible consequences afterward. This was true in Cuba. Succeeding generations would look upon that prosperous period as a time when the government should have diversified the economy, undertaken social welfare measures, educated the masses, and restricted the role of foreign (chiefly American) capitalism. Not a few voices in Cuba at that time advocated all of these policies. Literary figures such as Ramón Cabrera, José Antonio Ramos, and Carlos Loveira depicted social injustices. Enrique José Varona continued to preach, as did other professors and writers. Communists and other foreign-oriented radicals were heard, and so were public-spirited businessmen and members of the affluent classes. Such opinions counted for little during the 1920s. The government was depraved to an incredible degree during the entire decade and tyrannical toward the end of it. Cuba degenerated into a land of wretchedly poor administration, vice and immorality, low school enrollments, and a warped economy far too involved with that of its giant neighbor to the north. All was not gloom, of course, for many Cubans enjoyed prosperity and the benefits of the machine age as well as the spread of enlightenment through the press, radio, and motion picture. Still, it was a time of missed opportunity.

Some of the fault must be attributed to Dr. Alfredo Zayas y Alfonso, president from 1921 to 1925. "Doctor" by virtue of a law degree, he was an impassive man of some culture but widely regarded as lacking in character and moral courage. When he became president, conditions were little more than desperate because of the sharp post-war depression and the debauched Menocal administration. When his term was over, his few remaining followers pointed to the recovery of financial stability, a return of prosperity, an honorable relationship with the United States, and four years of freedom and order by Latin American standards. Yet Zayas' reputation was and remains low. He is arraigned not for tyranny but corruption even worse than that of his predecessors, for graft so brazen and pervasive that many Cubans, particularly the intellectuals, lost respect for the republic and abandoned hope of achieving progress through it.

When Zayas took office, General Crowder was in Havana as special representative of President Warren G. Harding, who had inherited him from the Wilson administration. Crowder's mission was to help stabilize the political situation and to ease the financial crisis, which had led to an almost total failure of banks and the defaulting of payment on Cuban bonds. In accordance with the "friendly neighbor" policy of Secretary of State Charles Evans Hughes, the United States was to support governments in power against revolutionists, to refrain from direct interference in internal affairs, but to employ financial aid to advance the commerce and investments of American nationals. Washington also hoped to moralize the Cuban regime through unofficial pressures, mainly the advice of General Crowder, and to cultivate the goodwill of the people. The surviving units of marines who had been stationed in Camagüey during the war were finally removed, and the Senate at last ratified the treaty of 1903 regarding Cuba's title to the Isle of Pines.

President Zayas at first had no option but to heed Crowder's counsel, since American financial support was necessary to run the government. Crowder fairly picked a "cabinet of honesty" for him in 1922 and secured the reduction of the Cuban budget by half, the dismissal of unneeded employees, levying of sales taxes, reform of the lottery, and cancellation of questionable contracts. This done, the United States sponsored a loan of $50 million through the Morgan bank, primarily to support the floating debt. Some Cubans objected not only to the tutelary aspects of Crowder's activities but to the drift of affairs that seemed to be reducing Cuba into a client state, a Haiti, through loans. Once the funds were in his hands, Zayas became an ardent nationalist. In April 1923 he dismissed part of the "cabinet of honesty" and a few months later the rest of it, informing the world that he was not challenging the United States but merely asserting his rights as president. The Cuban congress supported his action and asked the United States to abide by the Root interpretation of the Platt Amendment—by which there should be no interference in Cuba's internal affairs. There were influential Cubans who deplored Zayas' change of stance, stating openly that Crowder was a better friend of their nation than its own president. Crowder, who had become the first American to hold the rank of ambassador to Cuba in January 1923, was compelled to remain silent. United States policy was to continue to be cordial to the Zayas regime as part of a conciliatory Latin American strategy.

The carnival of nepotism and graft that followed established new records in a land that had been debauched by Spanish colonialism, Gómez, and Menocal. Cubans might add the name of Magoon. President Zayas typed out numerous messages and decrees, offering an impression of attention to duty, and called upon congress to pass various laws. But congress ignored him except for appropriations to build schools and roads that somehow failed to be constructed. The president's family and henchmen enjoyed fantastic opportunities for enrichment. Public services were performed badly if at all, and accounts for expenditures and receipts were so garbled that no one had a clear picture of the republic's finances. The so-called Tarafa Act, which sought to compel sugar growers to use the national railways, offered politicians a chance to exploit the cupidity of American owners of sugar plantations and the Consolidated Railway of Cuba. Bribery and blackmail were commonplace. One unusual action, however, was the passage of a law to establish pension funds for some occupations, though even this measure presented temptations to graft. American tourists contributed to the debased atmosphere by flocking to Havana during Prohibition for bouts of drinking and gambling. Gangsters and rumrunners also made their way to Cuba. Havana, with its traditions shaped by buccaneers, smugglers, corrupt rulers, and the long stopovers of Spanish fleets during colonial days, flourished as one of the most licentious ports on earth.

Meanwhile, the American bankers who had foreclosed on numerous Cuban sugar producers during the recent economic crisis were now expanding their holdings and modernizing the sugar mills and great *centrales*. By the middle of the decade United States interests controlled more than half of Cuba's sugarcane production. They were also buying heavily into electrical, telephone, and transportation systems. By 1924 the American investment in Cuba was $1,240 million, almost sixfold that of 1913. It occurred to no one in authority, apparently, that foreign holdings might be curbed. On the contrary, politicians and officials often made commissions by attracting the capital of outsiders. And, of course, Cuba was an underdeveloped land that needed such capital. Moreover, the chief distribution businesses and many small enterprises remained in the hands of Spanish nationals and other Europeans. Even the labor force was filling with aliens, since uncounted thousands of Jamaicans, Haitians, and Chinese were being imported to work for lower wages than Cubans received. Cuba was rapidly becoming an economic colony. While the Yankee would later be depicted as the villain in the process, he was encouraged by the elected Cuban government and he provided the money and means for its growth. Even had Washington wished to prevent the expansion of American holdings in the island, there was no legal way to do so.

Great sugar harvests and higher prices from 1922 to 1925 restored a surface prosperity to Cuba. The raising of American tariffs on Cuban imports in 1922, an action much protested in Havana, scarcely interfered with the lopsided development of the island's commerce. The United States purchased almost all of Cuba's exports and supplied two-thirds of her imports in 1924, though the recovery of Europe would soon alter this situation somewhat. Yet the commercial intimacy of the northern colossus to the island was overpowering by any standard. The Zayas regime smiled on it, rejoicing in the rising revenues and disposing of them in ways that gratified politicians.

Objections to the administration's ways began to be heard. The eminent historian and congressman, Fernando Ortiz, was instrumental in forming a committee for national and civic renovation. The Rotary Club of Havana took a responsible position in urging morality on the government. Julio Antonio Mella organized a secret Communist group which concentrated on university students who, though likely to be well-to-do, were often receptive. Calumnies against almost every public figure and the United States circulated widely, even though the bare facts were often damaging enough. A Veterans and Patriots Association, started to obtain bonuses and pensions for aging warriors of independence, soon became aggressive in attacking the administration. Many elements—decent, sinister, and selfish in motive—protested the lamentable state of the republic. Their list of accusations was long: tax frauds, graft in customs, abandonment of public works, lack of attention to charity and sanitation, prostitution, decline in education, corruption of the judiciary, employment of the army for political purposes, congressional inaction, illicit enrichment of officials, and unconstitutional actions by the president.

President Zayas was not a dictator, whatever his shortcomings, and he permitted a wide degree of outspoken public attacks. The Veterans and Patriots Association judged the time ripe for rebellion. On April 30, 1924, an uprising occurred at Cienfuegos. It was promptly put down, and the United States placed an embargo on arms and munitions that might reach other rebels and sold them to Zayas. As it happened, the insurrectionists had miscalculated the temper of public opinion and there were no further outbreaks. Zayas had promised that he would serve only one term. It is almost superfluous to record that he changed his mind as the elections of 1924 drew near, but his standing was so low that the Conservatives would not nominate him. Instead, they named former President Menocal, whose previous eight-year administration could be defended only in comparison to the recent one. Zayas threw the support of his small Popular Party to General Gerardo Machado, the Liberal nominee, and as president he was in a position to employ the bureaucracy and the army in such a way as to assure Machado's victory. Machado's slogan was "Water, roads, and schools," and he promised an extensive program of "moralization." The campaign was characterized by shooting affrays and other acts of violence, but the election itself went off comparatively peacefully. Machado won 200,000 votes to 136,000 for Menocal. Although the Conservatives had earlier threatened to revolt if they lost, Menocal broke precedent by admitting his defeat.

Dictatorship and Revolution (1925-1934)

It seemed a forlorn hope that the tawdry bureaucracy of Cuba might improve after Brigadier General Gerardo Machado y Morales took office as president in May 1925, but improve it did, so well that it became in two or three years an efficient instrument of tyranny. The army, police, and rural guards also enjoyed higher morale and better management. Machado may have been no worse as a man than his predecessors; he simply had more organizational ability. A native of Santa Clara, with little formal education, he had served well enough in the independence war to become one of the "in" group among the politicians who afterward ran the country. Once he was mayor of Santa Clara, and later a cabinet officer under Gómez. After that he had devoted himself mainly to business—to public utilities with American connections—and had become rich. His return to politics had shown him shrewd in manipulating men and attracting supporters. Somehow he had contrived to defeat Carlos Mendieta for the Liberal nomination in spite of Mendieta's greater popularity. The electoral campaign of 1924 against Menocal had been cleverly waged. A tall, corpulent man, Machado could be charming, frank, and gentle in manner when he chose. Never a genuine hero to the masses, he had qualities of strength and abilities that elicited respect from his compatriots.

A second "Dance of the Millions" was under way when Machado became president, with the *zafra* (sugarcane harvest) rising to 5,000,-000 tons by 1929. Prices were not particularly high, and the American market was in some jeopardy owing to competition from beet sugar and cane production in Hawaii, the Philippines, and Puerto Rico. Yet Cuba maintained its position as producer of 45 per cent of the world's sugar and as the supplier of half the United States' consumption. When American tariffs were raised in 1929, a well-heeled and persuasive lobby from the island won something of a victory in keeping the sugar duty increase down to one quarter of a cent. Machado was very friendly to American businessmen, who lionized him when he visited the United States in 1925 and 1927. Yet he realized that Cuba's economy was far too one-sided and that diversification was necessary. He sponsored a law in 1927 that provided tariff protection to certain Cuban industries. He also exhorted Cuban farmers to raise something besides sugarcane, though few heeded him.

The increased revenues that prosperity brought and the improved administration of Machado made a number of public works possible. Machado's pride was the construction of the great central highway, the *carretera*, which ran for 750 miles connecting the western tip of the island with the east. Even in this instance, however, it was necessary to borrow money from American banks. Numerous other roads created a network that enabled Cuba to share the benefits of the automobile age. Havana was much beautified by a new national capitol building, university construction, parks, and extensions of famous drives and boulevards. The provincial capitals were endowed with governmental palaces, street paving, aqueducts, and sanitation systems. As part of his diversification program, Machado created many schools for agriculture and technology. Laboratories and hospitals were built or expanded. The public education system received an improved curriculum, and many new buildings were constructed. Thousands of parent-teacher associations were formed throughout the island. Machado claimed that he purified the judiciary by removing corrupt judges, ending the scandalous sale of pardons, and introducing modern penology. In sum, Gerardo Machado seemed an able president during the prosperous years 1925-29. Washington as well as foreign business circles applauded him for the order and progress he had brought to Cuba. Ambassador Crowder, a high-minded expert on Cuban affairs, favored his reelection.

In counterpoint, it is clear that Machado neglected some of the island's fundamental problems. Much of the internal peace stemmed from his deportation of 400 labor "agitators" and such harsh coercion of others that President William Green of the American Federation of Labor protested. While some of the organizers were, as a Havana newspaper put it, agents of international totalitarianism who were trying to punish Cuba for crimes of the past committed in Siberia, Machado's policies curbed the growth of a healthy labor movement. And he erred fatefully in preventing the passage of a law that would have required all businesses to employ Cubans to the extent of three-fourths. To many, the island remained a paradise for foreigners, an orphanage for Cubans. American investors continued to purchase Cuban property, so that $1,500 million of it was in their hands by 1929. Latifundia, monoculture, and heavy reliance on foreign commerce and investment worsened under Machado, despite his efforts, largely verbal, to arrest the trend. Finally, his methods were more high-handed as time went on. Hangings in the rural areas and police brutality in the cities became more and more frequent.

Although Machado had made the customary promise that he would serve for only one term, that nothing could persuade him to extend it by a single day, his head was turned. He was so successful by 1927 that he won the mastery of the Conservative party organization and combined it with his own Liberal party and others. A constitutional "reform" was presently submitted, one by which the term of the president and congress would be extended by two years. After considerable criticism, some of it from Ambassador Crowder, a constitutional convention decided instead to go through with the election of 1928 but afterward to lengthen the terms. Machado paid a visit to Washington, where he inferred that President Coolidge did not regard the change as improper, and it was approved. In addition, the city of Havana became a central district under national control and the judiciary was implicitly subordinated to the executive, a damaging blow to the doctrine of separation of powers, for the courts had often displayed a spirit of independence. The congress was already the president's servant thanks to fear, bribes, and corrupt favors. Despite many irregularities in the way the constitutional change was made, Machado was reelected over virtually no opposition and was inaugurated for a six-year term in May 1929 before a sea of cheering Cubans.

More was involved than an effort to perpetuate a regime profitable to its favorites. Gerardo Machado was becoming a megalomaniac, taking seriously the praise of his supporters. He was strong and respected at home. His reputation abroad was high. He had played host with dignity to President Coolidge and the delegates of the Sixth Pan-American Conference in Havana in 1928 and received many fulsome testimonials. Now supremely self-confident, he planned to move in the direction of Mussolini in Italy, Primo de Rivera in

Spain, and Salazar in Portugal. Cuba would be safe for the property-owning classes and for foreigners, though it would stridently assert its nationalism, and it would enjoy discipline and internal peace. Machado himself would become an almost godlike figure with no opponents or critics.

Ironically, this prospect was foreclosed almost at its beginning. The Wall Street crash of October 1929 removed the underpinnings of Cuba's economy and opened a long period of depression. Foreign trade dropped until it was only one-tenth the 1929 level; American bankers who had competed to buy Cuban bonds were no longer available; and unemployment and bankruptcies brought misery. Government revenues fell by half. Hence many public employees were dismissed, others suffered salary cuts, and most were not paid at all for months at a time. Machado addressed himself to the crisis with his old energy, borrowing as much as he could abroad and curtailing imports. He embraced the Chadbourne plan, by which Cuba agreed to limit her sugar exports with the assurance that her competitors would also restrict theirs, but it failed to benefit the island. Both the price and output of sugar continued to fall. In truth, Machado could have done little to relieve his nation's condition. Better leaders than he of more fortunate countries than Cuba were also helpless before the depression. His army, now 12,000 strong and well-equipped, was still loyal, however, and despite the fall of several Latin American regimes in 1930 and a world-wide danger of revolution, Machado remained upright through some very difficult months.

Opposition to Machado had found a focus in the constitutional change of 1928, when a movement of "co-operativism" brought leaders of all shades together. Since Machado had absorbed both the Liberal and Conservative machines, his enemies had no organizations to channel their efforts and long seemed inept. Yet a new strain was showing, a compulsion to redress social injustices and to rid the island of its dependence on foreign, chiefly American, interests. However fine business conditions had seemed at times, most Cubans were poor and uneducated. Labor unions were frail and social welfare benefits appallingly inadequate. Communists and others had brought in fresh ideas from abroad and identified symbols for people to hate. Cuban educators and writers had been growing increasingly critical of the republic and the economic system. When the depression deepened, Cuba was full of social dynamite, and critics were available to light the fuses.

During 1930 it became evident that restlessness was widespread. Machado's American enthusiasts, who now had worries of their own with the depression, realized that Cuba was boiling. Members of the U.S. Congress aired complaints emanating from Cuba concerning the regime's severity. A student demonstrator was killed by the Havana police on September 30, 1930, an incident that caused an explosion of wrath all over Cuba and started an unending war between students and the regime. Machado closed the university and many high schools. Young people began to make impromptu speeches in public denouncing Machado, with predictable results. News stories were suppressed and foreign periodicals removed from the stands. A group of professors and students, among others, organized a terroristic group, the ABC, which threw bombs and grenades from moving automobiles at symbols of authority. Machado's gunmen, known as *porristas*, who had intimidated Cubans for some time, became more active than ever. Several killings were well-publicized: the president of the senate, the head of the secret police, and Julio Antonio Mella, the Communist organizer, whose assassination in Mexico was blamed on Machado, though it may have been a Stalinist execution. President Machado's own bathroom was mined. As Havana degenerated into a place of terror, the countryside became as lawless as it had been in the last days of Spanish rule. Yet Machado's army and police remained firm. He was strangely confident that the people still admired him. Once, before a crowd in Pinar del Río he offered to step down if his compatriots desired it, only to arouse a roar of protests.

Leaders whose claim to gratitude had little basis, like former President Menocal, came out openly against Machado and urged revolution, as did those who had better standing, such as Carlos Mendieta. In August 1931 these men engineered a landing in Pinar del Río from American hideaways, but they were badly defeated. At about the same time a youthful group in Oriente rose, also to be surrounded. There followed an intensification of terror. Machado's men shot prisoners thrown from automobiles, claiming they were trying to escape, and supposedly fed many opponents to sharks. Shots and bombs from automobiles, explosions in crowds, sniping from concealed places—these were rebel specialties. At times, Machado felt that he could safely pardon captured revolutionists, and did so in the ancient Spanish practice of alternating frightfulness with amnesty. But hatred for him grew. In the United States, his onetime admirers were saying by 1932 that he must go.

American policy under Coolidge had been to befriend Machado in the interest of Cuban stability, a condition that would presumably benefit Cuba as well as American business. Washington, which had been asked by the Cuban congress to observe the Root interpretation of the Platt Amendment, avoided intervention and announced that it would continue to do so. Under President Herbert Hoover and Secretary of State Stimson, American policy was even less inclined toward meddling. While many Cubans and American liberals did not realize it, Hoover's ambassador, Harry F. Guggenheim, favored abrogation of the intervention clause of the Platt Amendment and a public disavowal of Machado. Yet he was often regarded as an archetypal Wall Street conniver with Caribbean dictators and was sneered at as "Guggenado." As conditions both in the United States and Cuba deteriorated between 1931 and 1933, Washington offered little direction. Guggenheim and members of the American business community in Havana sometimes insisted to Machado that he call off the terrorism and compromise with his enemies. On at least two occasions Guggenheim offered his good offices in bringing the president to terms with Menocal and Mendieta, in vain. By the end of 1932 a strong revolutionary junta was set up in New York to direct the thousands of Cuban exiles in the United States and the underground in the island.

Soon after he took office, in 1933, President Franklin D. Roosevelt accepted Guggenheim's resignation and named a Caribbean expert from the State Department, Sumner Welles, as ambassador extraordinary to Cuba. At first Welles disclaimed any intention of unseating Machado. Rather, his mission was to pacify Cuba without resort to intervention and to alleviate her economic situation. He arrived in April and conferred with many influential persons in the island. By June he presented himself as mediator between Machado and the opposition. During July negotiations went on and rumors flew. Machado's temporary restoration of constitutional rights ironically permitted an outburst of public hostility toward him. A false report of his resignation filled Havana's plazas with cheering crowds early in August. A general strike followed. Welles presented Machado with an ultimatum to absent himself from the presidency for a period of deliberation. Machado refused, and seemed on the point of calling Welles' bluff for a few anxious hours. And then his generals abandoned him. In danger of losing his life, Machado flew to Nassau on August 12, 1933, narrowly escaping fire from ABC terrorists as his plane left the runway. For several years he wandered about the United States and the Caribbean, protesting that his record had been misrepresented and that he had served his country well.

Ambassador Welles and the revolutionary leaders shoved aside the general named by Machado as interim president and set up Dr. Carlos Manuel de Céspedes as provisional ruler. The United States recognized him, and he restored the constitution of 1901. This son of the first president of Cuba in the rebellion of 1868 had a famous name but little else. It was apparent that his position was shaky, mainly because of the economic crisis. Sugar had fallen to the lowest price within memory of persons then living, and the harvest of 1933 was only 2,000,000 tons. All over the island people were releasing their aggressions by killing the former agents of Machado. Rural bands were taking over sugar mills and threatening wealthy landowners and foreigners. In Havana, a student directory, composed of former or would-be university men, led organized agitation and rioting. It was obvious that Communist and socialist sentiments were popular among them. A multi-party group known as the Amalgam, which had long been developing doctrines of drastic social action outside the political structure, came out of hiding to ventilate left-wing nationalism. To such Cubans, as to many other peoples during the early 1930s, democratic republicanism seemed a failure. The appointment of Céspedes as president by the Yankee and the military appeared to be merely another instance of the frustration of Cuba's destinies by the sources who had caused her difficulties.

On the night of September 4, 1933 an astonishing event took place. Numbers of radical, hot-headed young people gathered at Camp Columbia, the principal army base near Havana, and met with hitherto circumspect representatives of the enlisted men. As it turned out, the dominant figure was a 32-year old sergeant named Fulgencio Batista y Zaldívar. At pistol point Batista arrested the army chief of staff and sat down at his desk. Deftly carrying through a plot he had devised, he quickly removed almost every army officer and took possession of Havana, whereupon a "pentarchy" of five leftists assumed the sovereignty of the nation. This body named Batista chief of the army with the rank of colonel. President Céspedes grumbled over his deposition but did not contest it with force, for he had none. Ambassador Welles was stunned by this turn of events. In a panic he called upon Washington three times within a few days to intervene with troops. Yet there was peace, with the populace rejoicing over events they scarcely understood, and President Roosevelt declined Welles' demands.

By September 10 the pentarchy disappeared, leaving one of its members as provisional president. This was Dr. Ramón Grau San Martín, a physician and professor of biology who had long been an idol to leftist university students. Grau abrogated the constitution of 1901 and, before cheering thousands in front of the presidential palace, proclaimed the beginning of social revolution. It was a wild period, full of promise and terror. American residents and wealthy Cubans were among those who feared the future. President Roosevelt and Secretary of State Cordell Hull were dismayed by the overthrow of Céspedes and attentive to Welles' importunities, but with the Good Neighbor policy already enunciated, they hesitated to answer appeals for intervention. Twenty-nine American warships, most of them small ones, were sent to Cuban waters to be on hand in case American lives were endangered. But Roosevelt and Hull would go no further. Nor would they recognize the regime of Grau San Martín.

For about a month the provisional president pushed ahead with his program to socialize Cuba by proclamation—by that only, for the government scarcely functioned and a renewal of disorders made life chaotic. Grau had a loyal following, but he also had enemies. His secretary of interior, Antonio Guiteras, became his rival in courting the more radical, Marxist-oriented elements. Colonel Batista was advancing enlisted men to the officerhood and solidifying his hold on the army. Even though it had shrunk to only 2,000 men, the army was the only cohesive force in the island. Its greatest test came when hundreds of deposed officers gathered with weapons in the Hotel Nacional in Havana, where Ambassador Welles stayed, and defied the new regime. After weeks of negotiation and blockade,

Batista removed them on October 2 by force, killing a number. His mastery of the army would remain unbroken for more than a decade. Batista was still willing to support President Grau. On October 10 Guiteras and the ABC withdrew from the government and agitated more violently than ever. On November 8 they sought to arouse Camp Columbia and revolutionize the streets of Havana. For a few hours they controlled much of the capital, but Batista subdued them and chased the ultraradical element into hiding or exile.

The Grau administration still displeased Welles, who persuaded his superiors with some difficulty that it was not effective and yet was potentially dangerous. Hull, who attended the Inter-American Conference at Montevideo in December 1933 and was heckled by a strident Cuban delegation, was eager to convince everyone that the United States was through with intervention. Thus he refused to send troops to Cuba. Nor would he recognize Grau's regime, despite British pressure and much common-sense evidence that it was viable. Early in 1934 Roosevelt, Hull, and the presidential representative who replaced Welles in Havana, Jefferson Caffery, indicated that they would never accept Grau. Colonel Batista was not slow-witted. Hints, or more, from American officials that he should remove the provisional president were comprehended. On January 14 he ousted Grau.

FERMENT, PROGRESS, AND A NEW ORIENTATION

The Revolution Tamed (1934-1952)

The deposition of Ramón Grau San Martín by Colonel Batista in January 1934 signified a decisive change in atmosphere. The revolution was not dead, but it would continue under the auspices of men who had little ideological purpose, mainly Batista. At first Carlos Hevia, a graduate of the U.S. Naval Academy, was named provisional president, but within thirty-two hours he quit because his name stirred so few supporters. Batista then installed Colonel Carlos Mendieta, a respected leader of the onetime Liberal Party who had political experience and was known to be a moderate. American recognition came with comic haste. Former President Grau, now in Mexico, was bitter that it took the United States such a short time to decide that Mendieta's rule was stable. In fact, conditions were almost as turbulent under Mendieta as they had been under Grau.

Although Mendieta issued a provisional constitution in February 1934 and organized a legislative Council of State, the political situation was still shaky. Strikes, riots, rebellions, and seizures of property battered at the authority of the new regime. Yet the revolution was past its peak.

Mendieta had the satisfaction of signing a treaty with the United States in May 1934 which replaced the hated Platt Amendment. Roosevelt had decided rather suddenly to make this change, which the American public and officialdom were quite ready for. The naval base at Guantánamo was retained. In August Cuba and the United States signed a reciprocity treaty which allowed most American goods to enter Cuba with little or no duty and gave Cuba a 22 per cent quota of the American sugar market at the very low duty of .9¢ per pound. The results of these two agreements were excellent at the time. Latin American distrust of the United States diminished as the most odious legal symbol of intervention was disowned. Cuba's sugar industry recovered markedly as both prices and production rose. And the benefits went increasingly to Cuban nationals, for American investors had been so injured by the great depression that the value of their holdings had shrunk from $1,500 million to about a third of that amount since 1929. Cubans were now recovering their predominance in their own major industry, many of them small or middle-sized owners. The Cuban share would rise rapidly, from 22 per cent in 1939 to 49 per cent by 1949. Furthermore, the increased revenues facilitated by reciprocity gave the government enough money to conduct its affairs, though many bonds were still in default. And American funds through the Export-Import Bank were available to relieve conditions if they became desperate. In short, the United States government replaced Wall Street as Cuba's financial supporter.

The general improvement in economic conditions probably stimulated a wave of strikes, as was happening in the United States in the middle 1930s. Yet some were the work of trouble-makers who hoped the Batista-Mendieta regime would fail, especially of Communists and *Auténticos*, members of a new party organized by followers of the socialistic former President Grau. In March 1935 it appeared that the economy would go to pieces as a result of labor disorders, many of which were politically motivated. A bloodbath at the hands of Colonel Batista on March 8 suppressed them. Soon afterward, Guiteras was killed, thus removing one of the principal sources of trouble. While snipers, bomb-throwers, and demagogues continued to make public life adventurous, the last half of 1935 witnessed a considerable calming of the island.

As general elections scheduled for January 1936 loomed, Cuban factions coalesced around unfamiliar new political organizations. Former President Menocal regrouped the old Conservatives as he ran for president, and Dr. Miguel Mariano Gómez, son of onetime President José Miguel Gómez, was the candidate of the Liberal survivors. In December 1935 Menocal charged that President Mendieta, a Liberal of yore, would weight the election in favor of Gómez, no doubt recalling how he himself had rigged the tests of 1916 and 1920. Mendieta honorably resigned and was succeeded by José A. Barnet, a diplomat who had been his secretary of state. Two aspects of the campaign attracted notice. Women were to vote for the first time in a presidential election, and despite the prominence of such names as Gómez and Menocal that aroused sentiments of the days of the revolution against Spain, it was obvious that the numerous Spaniards who had immigrated since independence were coming into their own as important political figures. Gómez won a clear victory in the election of January 1936.

The principal task of the administration was to prepare a new constitution. Its first test, however, was with Colonel Batista, whose appetite for power was growing as he indulged it. Batista had been very poor most of his life. Of mixed Spanish, Negro, and possibly Chinese ancestry, he had come from the cane-growing section of Oriente, worked as a tailor, barber, banana picker, and cane-cutter before taking to railroading, an occupation that afforded him a chance to see most of Cuba. Afterward he entered the army, where he managed to study with amazing determination. President Zayas had taken a liking to him and allowed him to use his library. Soon, Batista was a stenographer-secretary, in which capacity he learned much of the politics and inner workings of the military. A shrewd pagan, a man's man, laughing and affable, he had much appeal to the ranks of the army, and, eventually, to the Cuban masses. Hard as he could be, he was usually able to present the attractive side of his personality to the public with great success. Professing leftist sympathies, he seemed a peoples' natural hero during the 1930s.

Well aware of the importance of schooling, which had been so badly neglected, Batista devised a plan to create many rural schools under army direction, financing them by taxing bags of raw sugar. President Gómez perceived that Batista was in fact proposing an extension of the army's power and the development of a cult of himself among children. He indicated that he would veto the bill, whereupon congress, in December 1936, removed him from office for interfering with legislative prerogative. Not only had Batista unseated a recently elected president, but he had cheerfully disregarded hints that Washington did not want Gómez molested.

Vice-president Federico Laredo Bru now became president. Oddly, he crossed Batista on several minor occasions without losing his position. He brought about a more cordial mood in various ways, among them sponsoring an amnesty for nearly everyone, even Machado, who had been implicated in the crimes and disorders of the recent past. The Cuban congress passed an impressive body of welfare legislation —which has been ignored or minimized by supporters of Fidel Castro, who maintain that social amelioration was not thought of until 1959. Batista, of course, was behind these measures. His Three-Year Plan listed the customary points regarding improved public administration, health, sanitation, education, and public works found in all reformist programs. It went beyond them, however, in providing for massive unionization of labor in a great Confederation of Cuban Workers. And a law of sugar coordination of 1937 organized small farmers in cooperatives and agricultural workers in unions. Debt peonage was outlawed; tenant farmers were to be guaranteed an adequate share of the crop and were not to be deprived of their fields for any reason so long as they worked them. Although the law was not destined to be enforced at all times, it represented a marked advance. Furthermore, social security was extended to farmers and farm workers in 1941, and state lands were distributed to small growers. Meanwhile, legislation to provide pensions, insurance, limited working hours, and minimum wages largely satisfied the demands of the urban working classes. It was even decreed that the heads of all businesses in the island must be Cuban nationals. While the socialist revolution envisioned in 1933 was far from a reality, Cuba definitely turned the corner in the later 1930s in its move toward welfare statism.

Other currents during these years had their effects. Communists

were not obnoxious to Batista, who permitted them to operate more
or less freely. Pro-Franco Falangists and Nazis were also in evidence,
to no great discomfiture of the administration. These groups were
stridently anti-American, but so were most Cuban intellectuals on
their own initiative. There was less basis for this feeling now. Although President Roosevelt threatened in 1939 to raise duties on
Cuban sugar unless a settlement was reached regarding defaulted
bonds, he did not do so. Nor was the United States occupying as
overwhelmingly an important position in the Cuban economy as it
had before 1929. Yet anti-Americanism was fashionable among the
educated classes, even though it was largely ritualistic and typical of
a cultural lag between reality and the awareness of it by those who
should have been most alert.

After years of discussion, elections for a constituent assembly were
held on November 15, 1939. With only 57 per cent of the eligible
voters participating, the seven so-called Government parties won
558,000 votes but only thirty-five delegates; the Opposition Parties
had 551,000 votes and took forty-one delegates. Dr. Ramón Grau San
Martín was chosen president of the assembly when it convened in
February 1940. With noisy groups frequently invading the chamber
and demonstrating outside, there was much confusion. Yet the work
went on smoothly, with both Batista and Grau vying for favor as
the champion of the left. Batista came to terms with former President
Menocal and robbed the Opposition of its majority, a circumstance
that caused Dr. Grau to resign. The constitution was soon completed, however, and proclaimed from the capitol in Havana on
July 5.

It was a fine document, showing in many ways the maturity and
responsibility of Cuba's political leaders. The president was to serve
only one term, a provision that Franklin D. Roosevelt—of all people
—had suggested to Batista in 1938, though he might be reelected after
eight years. The cabinet should be partly responsible to congress, and
there would be a prime minister acceptable to both the president and
congress. Municipalities were given more freedom, and the judiciary
was restored to the independent position it had enjoyed under the
constitution of 1901. Many civil liberties and social welfare provisions
were defined at great length. Among the latter, workers were guaranteed paid vacations, minimum wages, and job tenure such that dis-

missal was virtually impossible. Homesteads were protected and co-operatives and unions strengthened. Industrialization was to be fomented, with safeguards favoring Cuban nationals over foreigners, and the acquisition of the sugar industry by Cubans made easier. One clause might have changed the nature of the social system had it been enforced: landholding was to be limited to 1,000 acres. In all, the constitution of 1940 was one of the most advanced in the world, and under it Cuba was to make striking progress. In contrast to the image presented by the revolutionists of the late 1950s, the island would have high standards of living and social justice compared to other Latin American or tropical lands.

Late in 1939 Batista resigned as chief of staff to become a candidate for president in the elections scheduled for July 1940. Accustomed now to power and wealth, he was more polished than the sergeant of 1933, but he still seemed a charismatic hero to the masses. His coalition, known as the Democratic Socialists, had Communist support. As nominee of the Cuban Revolutionary Party, or *Auténticos*, Dr. Grau again faced his old rival. Since the constitutional machinery was not fully established by July, the list of electors for president was confusing and probably many voters did not know for whom their ballots would be cast. Under these circumstances Batista won a signal victory. Yet he was probably the popular choice in any event. He settled comfortably into the president's chair and carried out his duties with appropriate dignity. With Dr. Carlos Saladrigas as his prime minister, he proceeded to govern as a strong president but not a dictator. An attempted coup by his chief of staff, Colonel José E. Pedraza, was suppressed with contemptuous ease, and internal order prevailed. The administration rounded out social welfare measures, stimulated the economy, and granted several rounds of wage increases to the working classes.

Soon after the United States became involved in World War II, Cuba declared war, on December 9, 1941. Air and naval bases were made available to the Americans, and Cuba participated in naval patrols in the Gulf and Caribbean, during the course of which she lost a number of ships. The war also spelled shortages of finished goods and some types of food in the island, but generally it brought benefits. The United States was liberal with loans and grants; Americans helped improve Cuban facilities and increase production of such minerals as nickel and cobalt; and Cuban pride was gratified by representation in various international conferences. As in World War I, Cuba's principal role in the war effort was to produce sugar. The United States purchased all Cuban sugar after domestic consumption at 2.65¢ per pound, with duties set at .75¢. This arrangement lasted from 1942 through 1947. It was, of course, very advantageous to Cuba, whose production advanced to 5,000,000 tons a year.

Though Batista was a strong president and enjoyed wartime powers, he did not rule as an autocrat. Confident that the propertied classes supported him, he cultivated labor and pleased the left by establishing diplomatic relations with the Soviet Union in 1943 and by giving two Communists cabinet rank. The elections of 1944 revealed that he was not as successful as he imagined. His familiar opponent, Dr. Grau, received 924,000 votes to 720,000 for Dr. Saladrigas, the heir of Batista and nominee of the government coalition. Batista took the rebuff gracefully and went on a good-will tour of South America, where he praised democracy repeatedly. Then he settled in the United States in exceedingly comfortable circumstances.

Dr. Ramón Grau San Martín inherited a wartime boom that soon became another "Dance of the Millions" as sugar production and prices rose after 1945. He was also the benefactor—after due overturns under the spoils system—of as competent a bureaucracy as Cuba had known since the American occupation. Regarded as a stalwart leftist and anti-American of the old school, an archetypal economic nationalist, Grau was expected to reorient Cuba's political and economic life. Yet he was not equal to the opportunity he had so long coveted. His administration was a sad affair, a carnival of graft and irresponsibility. War and postwar shortages encouraged black markets, which usually corrupted officialdom. A flood of American tourists to Havana stimulated long-established traditions of catering to gambling instincts and vices. Extravagance and immorality seemed to affect all classes.

Furthermore, Grau had much difficulty with the Communists. Finding Mexico inhospitable after the end of the Lázaro Cárdenas administration in 1940, the international Communist apparatus made Havana its headquarters for Latin America. Communists were so active in labor unions that disputes and strikes were almost chronic, and student riots, such as those involving young Fidel Castro, were often violent to a murderous degree. President Grau rather pathetically attempted to conciliate the Communists—and then to break their power over labor—but only alienated many of his supporters and made the Communists bolder. Congress was unwilling to cooperate with him, with the result that he employed heldover wartime powers to issue thousands of decrees of dubious constitutionality and propriety. In these actions he almost invariably favored nationals over foreigners and labor over management. Yet turbulence among the working classes and agitation among the students worsened. Unofficial armed bands took it upon themselves to bring disorder and violence into labor disputes in the countryside. Political assassinations—in one year fifty were recorded—further disrupted civilized life. Gangsterism, whether criminal or political, was clearly out of hand.

It has always puzzled Grau San Martín's onetime admirers that he permitted or even encouraged such disorders. Perhaps Sumner Welles' low opinion of him in 1933 was not so unjustified after all. Equally surprising was Grau's attitude toward peculation. Enormous public works were begun and left unfinished, the politicians having pocketed the funds. The president himself was extravagant to a shocking degree, as was his official family. The rapid growth of Havana's luxury hotels, bordellos, gambling casinos, night clubs, and flamboyant homes mocked the austere socialist standards that Grau had long extolled. It was a symbolic joke when someone stole a great diamond embedded in the floor of the national capitol and, after a few days, placed it on the president's desk. During these years, as in the 1920s, many young Cubans developed a contempt for materialists and politicians, among them a troublesome student named Fidel Castro.

As the elections of 1948 approached, Cuban parties were splintered. Dr. Carlos Prío Socarrás, an *Auténtico*, was the heir of President Grau, though he clearly had many reservations about his sponsor. Eduardo Chibás, the famous "Eddy" of regular radio broadcasts who kept an enormous following titillated by alleged exposures of scandals, had organized an *Ortodoxo* Party in protest against Grau's leftist and corrupt policies. The Communists, who called themselves Popular Socialists, entered a candidate, Juan Marinello, and a catch-all coalition nominated Ricardo Núñez Portuondo. On election day Prío Socarrás won with a total of 900,000 votes, though he had less than a majority of the total cast.

A lawyer of youthful good looks from Pinar del Río, Prío Socarrás took office in October 1948. He had been a hot-headed student rebel under Machado and had gone to jail. In September 1933 he was one of the promoters of the Batista coup at Camp Columbia, and he had been a shrill member of the Cuban delegation at the Montevideo conference of 1933-34. Afterward, Prío had served in various high positions, lately as a cabinet minister under Grau. Now he hoped to restore effective administration, end violence, and remove Communists from positions where they could do mischief. He succeeded in none of these aims. Overenthusiastic labor organizing—or racketeering and gangsterism—continued as before, discouraging honest business. Foreigners no longer cared to invest in Cuba except for buying utility bonds. Cuban capital went abroad or into tangible property. Prío puzzled foreigners by dealing with suspected Communists and supporting the Caribbean Legion, whose purpose was to overthrow governments. Yet his relations with the United States were extremely good except for a few weeks in 1949 after a few American sailors desecrated the statue of José Martí in Havana. Prío's prosecution of former President Grau San Martín for embezzling $174 million indicated a moral victory of public honor over political debt, but the curious destruction of evidence and consequent abandonment of the trial suggested the reverse.

A report on Cuba by the International Bank for Reconstruction and Development (IBRD) threw much light on conditions in 1949 and 1950. Drift, corruption, and irresponsibility characterized the government. The bureaucracy was inefficient and overstaffed, with workers suffering from job insecurity. On the other hand, labor had too much job security, for it was almost impossible to discipline or dismiss anyone. Congress rarely voted budgets, which were irregularly gotten up; there was no auditing or control on executive spending. Cuban taxes were rather high by Latin American standards, but evasion was common. Education had been shamefully neglected from the early days of Machado until Prío, who had attempted to restore the public system and had established two new universities. In general, however, teachers were unqualified political appointees who often drew their salaries without performing any service. One informant of the IBRD mission described the teaching profession as a nest of criminals and scoundrels. Prío's minister of education loaded many millions into a truck and drove to the airport, where he took a plane to Florida and declared himself a refugee. Illiteracy among the adult population had long hovered at about 40 per cent. Perhaps Prío's efforts resulted in its reduction to 25 per cent, as he claimed, by 1953.

The IBRD report pictured the sugar industry as the mainstay of the economy, though it was not keeping pace with scientific advantages then available. Half of it was now owned by Cubans, for American interests had been declining since 1929. The Korean War had stimulated sugar sales and commerce in general, but the dependence of the island on the American market for sugar was an unwholesome situation. Cubans could easily have diversified their agriculture to a considerable degree had the government provided leadership. Light industries were expanding, but they would have grown much faster if political conditions were better. Livestock-raising and fishing needed official encouragement and modern methods. Tourism was a huge business, with 150,000 foreigners visiting the island in 1949 in addition to 30,000 excursionists who stopped over. Yet facilities were lacking except for tourists who sought entertainment and frivolous pleasures, and the income that Cuba derived from this source was almost cancelled out by the expenditures of Cubans who traveled abroad. In all, the IBRD report revealed that Cuba was missing many opportunities, largely because of her ineffective government and lack of initiative by her citizens. Cuban intellectuals, however, usually blamed the United States for the failure of the island to realize its potentialities.

While Prío Socarrás had exerted little leadership, he had restored a more cordial atmosphere through amnesties and conciliation. Among those who came home at this time was former President Fulgencio Batista, who had prudently chosen to live abroad during the Grau administration, and had lived very well on a fortune he had acquired somehow. Elected to the senate, the heavier and more mellow ex-sergeant did not seem dangerously ambitious when he put together a coalition and announced his candidacy for the presidency in 1952. The *Ortodoxos* had been very critical of President Prío Socarrás and were prepared to wage a vigorous campaign. They lost their leader, however, when "Eddy" Chibás shot himself after a radio broadcast in 1951 in which he had failed to adduce evidence he had promised would disgrace the administration. He died shortly thereafter. The *Ortodoxos* thereupon nominated Roberto Agramonte, a sociology professor and influential writer. With Prío's blessing, the *Auténticos* chose Carlos Hevia, who had been president briefly in 1934, to carry the banner for the government coalition. The issues centered on charges by Agramonte and Batista condemning the administration for peculation, gangsterism, and neglect of duty. It seemed that Hevia would probably win, though Agramonte might have a chance.

A False Revolution—and a True One (1952-1959)

The campaign had scarcely begun when, early on March 10, 1952, Batista settled matters by driving into Camp Columbia and carrying out a coup even more smoothly than he had in 1933. Within two hours Batista men were in charge of the armed services and police at all key spots. No one was killed. Isolated, President Prío headed for the Mexican embassy and asylum. Batista explained to the people that Prío had been planning to call off the elections and set up a dictatorship. International recognition for the new provisional president came readily from all except the Communist bloc, which Batista defied from the outset. Even though a coup of this type was unique in the history of the Cuban republic, Batista had a good reputation abroad. Cubans knew him better than foreigners did and were well aware that he had learned and forgotten much since the days when he had been a hero to the working classes. Rejoicing over his return was restrained.

Despite a bout of chicken pox that curbed his activities for a few days, Fulgencio Batista quickly formed a new regime. Suspending the constitution of 1940, largely his own handiwork, he set up a consultative council of eighty members to replace congress and dissolved all political parties. Although a few persons were jailed or threatened, freedom of expression was not seriously curtailed. Students rioted frequently, political leaders issued manifestoes and spoke in public, and newspapers—even though subsidized in part by the government, as had been customary since 1935—published what they wished. Batista soon had the armed services and police contented by pampering which he knew so well how to administer, and they greatly reduced the disorders that had long rent the island. Urgency courts, agencies with which Cubans were familiar in crises of the past, made it easier for Batista to punish political enemies whose rights might have been respected more scrupulously by the regular judiciary. Public services were considerably improved, though corruption was far from eradicated.

Batista repeated his feat of the 1930s in winning over the major labor leaders as well as the rank and file. Though economic conditions were shaky for a few months after the coup, they soon responded to internal peace, encouragement to foreign investors and traders, and wage hikes. A sugar stabilization fund Batista set up helped prevent a ruinous drop in prices as the world market sagged because of over-production. A record sugar production of 7,000,000 tons had been reached in 1952; now it was to be cut to 5,000,000 tons. Public works and the creation of numerous small industrial establishments saved Cuba from a period of depression that had seemed inevitable. Prosperity was to be a mark of the Batista years; reform and social justice were destined to be victims.

Batista's enemies were unforgiving about the coup of 1952, which to be sure was not justified by any true crisis. Chief among them was deposed President Prío Socarrás, who had access to enormous funds which financed gun-running, bribes, and anti-Batista propaganda. Since the older politicians quarreled riotously among themselves, the dynamics of the new revolutionary movement centered about students and miscellaneous groups probably aided by Prío. During the spring of 1953 rumors indicated that a major attempt to unseat Batista was imminent. Not until July 26 did a revolt break out. Almost two hundred young men assaulted the Moncada Barracks near Santiago de Cuba while risings occurred in scattered parts of the island. The effort was a miserable failure, but it stirred the population and destroyed the serenity of the regime. It turned out that the leader of the Moncada attack was Fidel Castro Ruz, a 26-year-old doctor of laws who had long been involved in terrorism and intrigue in Cuba and abroad. Castro's personal heroism on this occasion has been furiously debated. Soon after, he was arrested and sentenced to fifteen years in prison by a court at Santiago de Cuba which freed a third of his companions. At the conclusion of his trial Castro delivered an impassioned, self-righteous harangue which was widely publicized, his final words, "History will absolve me," becoming a slogan. By propaganda methods that are still imperfectly understood, he became almost overnight a martyr and a myth.

Batista was shaken enough by the affair to proclaim a 90-day state of siege and to clamp down savagely on the island's liberties. By the beginning of 1954 the siege was over and business was booming. The United States government arrested Prío Socarrás for shipping weapons to Cuba. After many delays, he was fined by an American court. It seemed that the danger of revolution had passed. Batista organized a Progressive Action Party and ran for president against his old foe, Grau San Martín, who withdrew shortly before the election of November 1954 on the grounds that it would be rigged. Though voting was obligatory, only half the electorate cast ballots. In February 1955 Batista was inaugurated for a four-year term, and constitutional government was nominally restored.

A general amnesty freed most of the political prisoners in May, including Fidel Castro, who returned triumphantly to Havana and then departed for Mexico on unspecified business. Former President Prío came back to Cuba, to serve as a focus of discontent and a financier of rebellion. The press was almost entirely free to criticize Batista. He was also denounced volubly in mass meetings that attracted thousands during the fall of 1955. Although both the familiar leaders of the past and the new generation opposed the regime, the country was calm. Times were good, with bank deposits and reserves the highest on record. Cuba was one of the few countries to check inflation, and her population growth was not explosive. Commerce and tourism flourished. The decline in sugar production, which the government had planned, was more than offset by the creation of new industrial plants and some diversification of agriculture. And there was so much construction in Havana and other cities that the face of Cuba was almost transformed. Cubans had the highest standard of living of any tropical nation—one of the four highest in Latin America. Since the beginning of the republic their society had been unusually fluid, with movement from one class to another relatively easy. Furthermore, most of the prosperity of the 1950s favored Cubans, not the Yankee of caricature, though a cultural lag among the intellectuals caused the images of the 1920s to persist.

The Batista regime waxed fat and complacent. It was no secret that the president, his official family, and the bureaucracy, army, and police performed their duties casually and enriched themselves energetically. But this condition had always prevailed in Cuba and was not as pronounced under Batista as it had been in other administrations. The worst feature of the situation was the neglect of social problems. Though Cuba's percentage of poor persons was as small as that of any Latin American land, the number was still dangerously high in an age of rising expectations. Familiarity with better conditions in the United States and the rapid improvement of some segments of the Cuban population made the others restless and clamorous. Perhaps Batista, who had done so much for the working classes in the past, had run out of ideas or no longer cared. He may have believed that continuing prosperity and judicious favors to labor leaders would solve the problem of poverty in time. Other people demanded more drastic action. Chief among them were Communists, who probably numbered from ten to twenty thousand but who could, and did, attract tenfold their numbers in free elections. Like Latins in both European and American countries, many could announce themselves Communists on Monday, non-Communists on Tuesday, and anti-Communists on Wednesday without undergoing serious intellectual or psychological stress. Such citizens nonetheless received a great deal of indoctrination. Other Cubans, mainly educated and responsible people, had never admired Batista or accepted his coup of 1952. To them the regime was a do-nothing administration, a backward-looking government of racketeers and profiteers that drifted further each day from the mainstream of world forces.

Although 1956 was generally a satisfying year for Batista, an event in December started his plunge to disaster. Fidel Castro and eighty-one other revolutionists who had been training in a Mexican hideout with professional Communists and bizarre adventurers sailed in the launch "Granma" to the southeastern coast of Cuba. The government had anticipated the invasion and managed to apprehend all but a dozen of the party soon after the "Granma" was beached. Fidel Castro, his brother Raúl, and an Argentine physician, Ernesto ("Che") Guevara, were among the few who escaped into the cliffs and woods of the Sierra Maestra. Risings in other parts of the island failed to come off on schedule, and it was announced that Castro had been killed.

By the spring of 1957 it was apparent that the revolutionists were very much alive, indeed were beginning what would later be judged one of the most fateful political campaigns in the history of the New

World. The rugged hideaway gave the group perfect isolation from airplanes or soldiers. Castro was soon making use of a radio sending station and a printing press, as well as weapons, funds, and an island-wide network of confederates. The discovery that he was alive—by Herbert L. Matthews of *The New York Times*—was a much less epochal event than admirers and critics of Matthews have judged. Castro and the well-experienced revolutionists in his circle had skills and allies enough to make the "Movement of the 26th of July" formidable without the favorable publicity abroad provided by the influential New York journal. He was to win by capturing the minds of Cubans, not those of foreign enthusiasts. Propaganda was soon being circulated all over the island and bombs were destroying schools and motion picture houses. The Batista regime was presently so much on the defensive that Church and labor leaders were professing their neutrality. Terrorism was an old story in Cuba; its sudden revival in 1957 after five years of calm indicated a reversion to familiar habits. Yet there was something more: Castro had advocates in the island and abroad who sprang up to advertise the notion that he was an authentic folk hero who personified the hopes of the common men of Latin America.

In March 1957 a mass attack on the presidential palace proved to be a close call for Batista, who was in great danger for a few minutes. A much larger group gathered to cheer him on the following day, but thereafter he was careful not to expose himself to assassination. Student turbulence became so violent that the universities and most superior schools were shut down. Censorship was now very strict. Successive states of siege authorized the government to take the harshest of repressive measures. Batista concentrated forces in Oriente province, but they could not penetrate the rebel territory in the Sierra Maestra and many soldiers sold their weapons to Castro or defected. By air and sea, supplies and equipment reached the insurrectionists, much of it from the United States. Exiles swarmed out of the country as its atmosphere recalled the times of Weyler and Machado. Though 1957 was to prove one of the best years economically in the island's history, Cuba was in a desperate condition. The regime had no moral authority, and the rebels were still surrounded.

The year 1958 opened with the *zafra*, the sugarcane harvest, being ahead of schedule to avoid the burnings of cane threatened by Castro.

Sabotage increased, as did police brutality, jailings, and beatings. Castro's propaganda grew more effective. It became a great game for foreign journalists to visit the bearded, cigar-smoking leader in daring incursions into the mountains. He was usually represented to the world as a sincere but cloudy idealist who loved to deliver lengthy monologues on social injustices. Seldom did he fail to include remarks that would suggest that he was not a Communist. Already a living legend, Castro refused to work with other political groups, notably the exiles who had set up a junta in Miami. This attitude was praised as a moral virtue, an indication that the Movement of the 26th of July spurned the discredited politicians of the past. Now and again someone who knew him well would insist that Castro was a dedicated Communist, but most people doubted it, and the leader himself scornfully denied that he was.

By the spring of 1958 it was unsafe for buses and trains to operate on schedule in many parts of Cuba because of armed attacks. Tourists almost stopped going to Cuba. A cowardly campaign of bombing schools practically ended public education. Soldiers and officials were in danger of assassination if they did not cooperate with the revolutionists. In April, Castro called a general strike of the sort that had toppled Machado in 1933. As if in preparation for the fall of Batista, the United States cancelled all shipments of arms to the Cuban government, even those that had been paid for. The bishops publicly called upon Batista and Castro to effect a compromise and prevent further terrorism. Yet the strike failed. Batista's armed supporters, probably 40,000 strong, were still loyal and effective; so were his bemused labor leaders; and because they were not allowed to control the strike, the Communist hierarchy did not participate. For a few weeks it looked as though Castro had staked everything on the general strike and had lost. Batista smugly went ahead with plans for the election of November 1958, in which his candidate, Andrés Riva Agüero, was to oppose Grau San Martín of the *Auténticos* and Carlos Márquez Sterling of the *Ortodoxos*.

Castro threatened death to anyone who ran for office and terror for those who went to the polls. His movement recovered momentum by the kidnaping of American businessmen and servicemen, all of whom were released after angry official protests but rather jocular publicity in the world press. Castro's victory at home and abroad was all but complete by the autumn of 1958. Having won first the rural population, he attached the business and professional classes, and finally captured the urban proletariat, all the time enjoying favorable attention in the outside world. All that stood before him now were the army and police of Batista. The United States was no obstacle to him, much as this idea has become imbedded in the myth of the revolution. Washington had no intention of aiding Batista or of intervening. Those who made the decisions—President Eisenhower, Secretaries of State Dulles and Herter, and Ambassador Earl T. Smith—had scant use for Batista by 1958, if not sooner. They wanted a freely elected administration to assume power peacefully when the dictator's term ended, in February 1959, and of course to prevent a bloodbath in the island. To the impassioned followers of Castro this attitude may have seemed hostile. Second-level policy-makers in the American department of state virtually supported Castro and were eager to hasten Batista's fall.

The election of 1958 proved a farce, with Riva Agüero winning a one-sided victory. Those who favored Castro or other candidates feared or scorned to vote. Still hoping to avoid identification with either Batista or Castro, the United States government sought to persuade Cuban leaders to form a caretaker regime and hold fresh elections. But things had gone too far. Castro's forces had burst out of the Sierra Maestra and entered the Sierra del Cristal and the province of Las Villas. Batista made one last desperate effort to destroy the revolutionists. His army swarmed into the affected areas, only to surrender or melt away. After a sober New Year's Eve gathering at Camp Columbia, Batista suddenly flew off. Thousands of his partisans crowded the airports and docks to flee into exile. Early on January 2, 1959, Che Guevara arrived in Havana with 600 insurgents and took over the capital.

The Batista regime had lost the respect of the people and had collapsed. Castro's guerrilla forces had not bested the soldiers in the field, nor had crowds in the cities overpowered the authorities. Economic conditions had not driven a maddened population to revolt; on the contrary, they had been rather good, and many of Castro's most ardent followers were well-to-do. Psychological factors mainly explain the triumph of the revolution. The same publicity skills that had made the Movement of the 26th of July appear heroic and purifying had given Batista one of the most odious reputations in the world. In justice, it should be reiterated that he was by no means the worst ruler that Cuba had endured. If Batista was no monster, at least in comparison with other Caribbean tyrants, he was nonetheless a hard and ruthless autocrat who had resorted to torture and other barbarities to prolong his power. His administration itself was born of unjustified rebellion. It had been unedifying and cynical, careless of national pride, insincere in advocating social justice, and ineffective in dealing with the country's problems.

Although the same charges could be made against almost every Cuban president, the timing in Batista's case was fatal. By 1959 nationalism had become a malignant force in underdeveloped lands like Cuba, just as it was playing itself out in the more advanced ones. It turned naturally against the United States as the smothering giant who had kept the island in thralldom, disregarding the patent fact that nearly every constructive material achievement in Cuba was derived from its intimacy with the northern neighbor. Since the basic principles of Marxism, broadly defined, had become, as David Burks states, the unspoken assumptions of Cuban intellectual life, those who exerted the most influence on youth could concentrate hate on Uncle Sam as Communism's principal foe and Cuba's national oppressor. The Soviet Union, on the other hand, was depicted as a fundamentally benevolent and peace-loving power. Even though Batista had often dealt with Communists, he pretended to defy them, probably to please Washington, and by 1957 they ceased collaborating with him. The precipitate drop in his prestige was largely due to the skill of Marxists and nationalists in labeling him a creature of the Yankee.

Fidel Castro in Power (1959-   )

During January 1959, when most of the population exulted over the revolution, there was no consensus as to its meaning. Castro's rambling monologues may have been brilliant hortatory feats in inspiring the masses to demand drastic changes in society, but they lacked coherence. Written statements put out in the name of the 26th of July Movement were, like most political platforms, full of promises for everybody. Essentially, Castro was committed to political democracy and social reform. There was basis for believing that he represented a new, young Cuba that would sweep away the corrupt morass of the republic and introduce a puritanism that José Martí had advocated. Castro had indicated that he favored a partnership of Cuban and foreign technology and capital. He had kind words for religion, liberty, and international obligations. Repeatedly, he promised to hold honest elections. The middle classes had early accepted him as a freedom-loving reformer who would probably do nothing more than advance Cuba along the path of economic nationalism. Urban labor was already favored but might expect more benefits. Rural workers, especially the *guajiros* who labored in the canefields part of the year, were greatly stirred by indications that the long-neglected provisions of the constitution of 1940 for land distribution would make them owners. The major property holders were nervous, but Castro's threats had scarcely gone beyond conventional political oratory.

Hope dominated the air far more than dread, though occasional voices of warning were heard. Castro, these said, was a maniac, a fanatical egotist, and as false a man as ever scaled the heights to power. Not a few persons claimed to know that he was, and had been for years, a dedicated Communist. His plans for Cuba, or what could be made of them from conflicting utterances, did not justify such fears. Rather, they stimulated widespread hopes that here was a maker of one of the epochal revolutions of world history, one to rank with that of France in 1789 or Mexico in this century. The aura of the movement enraptured idealists all over the planet. There was a sense of anticipation that the bearded young leader would bring out the best in Latin America and set a benign pattern for its future.

Whatever his true essence, Castro's personality overwhelmed Cuba. This lovable man of 32, cigar-smoking and nonchalant, filthy, athletic, and carelessly clad—but intellectual—had the rare quality of projecting himself to the masses in such a way as to enslave them. Rational people were caught up in hysterical devotion as they saw him. They listened entranced for hours while he exulted and ranted, and responded with delight to his common touch. Not a great deal was known of the man, and information was contradictory. His father was a Spaniard who had come to Cuba poor but had acquired substantial sugar and livestock properties. He had remained crude in his habits and difficult to deal with. Fidel, Raúl, and three others were products of an illicit union of the elder Castro and a servant girl he eventually married. The illegitimate Castro children resented the two older, legitimate ones, but in time they also quarreled with their mother and among themselves. Fidel had gone to a Jesuit school and then to the University of Havana, where he exhibited considerable academic ability. During the late 1940s his activities had been controversial. A wild, unstable beatnik, he may have been involved in murders and attempted assassinations of a political nature. He participated in the futile Cayo Confites expedition of 1947 to overthrow Dictator Trujillo of the Dominican Republic. Castro had been present at the notorious *bogotazo* of 1948, when hideous riots almost destroyed the capital of Colombia. Testimony is contradictory about his role there. A riot monger and trouble-maker while a student, he finished his degree in law in 1950 and married. After Batista's 1952 coup he involved himself with various adventurers, some of them Communists, and traveled in the United States and Central America on mysterious errands. The attack on the Moncada Barracks in 1953 made Castro a hero to Cuban youths, and he strengthened his ties with them by an extensive correspondence during his imprisonment of almost two years on the Isle of Pines. His ovation in Havana after the amnesty, his journey to Mexico, and return on the "Granma" in December 1956 acquired an epic character as *fidelistas* related them. Yet many sordid episodes and accusations of betrayal marred his career. Obviously, he was dedicated and determined. If he was greedy he craved power and glory rather than wealth, and he repeatedly overcame obstacles that ordinarily defeat men.

Castro's progress from Oriente to Havana was a triumph of an almost religious character. Hailed as a messiah and deliverer, he also posed as an avenging deity along the way by ordering the summary execution of Batista partisans. Havana on the day of entry, January 8, 1959, was in a state of delirium. Swarms of unknown men moved into the capital, ousting soldiers and officials, taking over homes and hotels. They seemed young, rustic, fanatical, and, on their leader's orders, abstemious. It was their faith that made them attractive. It was understandable that confusion marked the new government, which Castro had set up in Santiago de Cuba, with Miguel Urrutia Lleo as president and José Miró Cardona as premier. Fidel claimed no official position. International approval of the new regime was almost unanimous, and recognition came promptly. While the mal-treatment of *batistianos* marred the highly favorable foreign reaction, most observers were inclined to excuse the vengeance wrought upon such supposedly beastly characters. In the wave of good humor and optimism that accompanies revolutions, it was easy to believe that Castro and his men spoke from the heart of Latin America and that they would earnestly try to bring about a utopia.

Fidel exulted in his personal adulation and exhausted himself stim-ulating it. He flew off to Venezuela for another accolade, but some-how he alienated President Rómulo Betancourt, whom so many liberals regarded as representative of the best aspirations of Latin America and who had earlier helped Castro. When José Figueres, former president of Costa Rica and another idol of the non-Commu-nist left, came to Havana in March he was insulted before a large audience by Castro. Meanwhile, public trials for the "criminals" of the fallen regime were conducted as spectacles before jeering crowds shouting *paredón* (to the wall—to be shot). At least 550 former officials and soldiers were so tried and killed within the first few weeks. Presently, on February 15, Miró Cardona ceased to be premier. Fidel Castro replaced him, and his brother Raúl became commander of the armed forces. The national lottery was converted into a device to finance housing projects, and on-the-spot land division was begun with maximum publicity in Oriente and Pinar del Río. It was a hectic time, thrilling and disturbing. Developments came so fast that a previous week's information was likely to be out of date. The only clear continuity was provided by Castro himself, who appeared un-predictably anywhere to delight the people and, usually nightly, was on television to teach, preach, inspire, and threaten.

In April the Cuban leader accepted an invitation from the Ameri-can Society of Newspaper Editors to visit the United States. But for a few pickets, his reception was cordial in the extreme. Americans had generally accepted the assurances of popular writers—there were few experts on Cuba—that the island had long been kept in a "feudal" condition by great landlords, mostly American, and that the ragged peasants photographed with Castro were typical of the population. The magnetic hero played his part well; he was the sincere idealist and man of reason. Cuba, he stated, did not seek help from any foreigner, but a Marshall Plan for Latin America would be wise. He insisted that his "heart was with the West" in its struggle with Communism and that neither he, Raúl, nor anyone else in the regime was a Communist. It is not certain what transpired when Castro and his party talked with Secretary Herter and Vice-President Nixon. The Americans probably made tentative offers to assist Cuba but did not beg for the privilege of doing so, an attitude that must have offended Castro. Nixon concluded that he was probably a Communist. Afterward, it became an article of faith to many that the United States missed a chance to win over the Cuban revolution by not helping it at that stage.

Following his triumphs in the United States, Castro pleased crowds in Montreal, flew over Havana to favor his people with a radio broadcast, and then continued to Buenos Aires, where he was applauded for suggesting that the United States supply $30 billion to develop Latin America. For a man who two years before had camped in the Sierra Maestra with a small, isolated following, such international acclaim must have been heady.

A significant chord sounded in May 1959 when an agrarian law was presented. In effect the measure turned over to the state the right to confiscate and operate all landed property. It was so drastic that five cabinet members resigned, and the United States expressed concern in a diplomatic note. Perhaps the fatal breach between the moderates and the radicals occurred at this point. While the reform was being debated, the Communists tried and failed to win control of the labor organization in union elections, and Castro denounced them as antirevolutionary. Whether he was obscuring the implications of the agrarian law with gestures, or whether elements in the regime were working at cross-purposes is a matter of dispute. In June the agrarian law was proclaimed. It soon became apparent that former owners were not to be compensated, but also that few *guajiros* were to become independent farmers. Rather, confiscated plantations and estates were made into state farms or cooperatives managed by a National Institute of Agrarian Reform. By 1964 the cooperatives would all but disappear, and 70 per cent of Cuban agriculture would be state-owned. Production in almost every category fell drastically between 1959 and 1964, and much food was rationed.

A spate of defections caused an uproar during the summer of 1959. The air force commander, Pedro Díaz Lanz, left the island, charging that Communists were taking it over. One of Castro's oldest associates, Major Huber Matos, was sent to prison for trying to escape. The provisional president of the republic, Manuel Urrutia, a onetime judge who had lost his position for befriending Castro in 1953, quit after Castro threatened to resign before a protesting crowd. Carlos Márquez Sterling, leader of the *Ortodoxos*, asked for asylum, and onetime President Grau San Martín was dismissed from the university. Cuban diplomats abroad resigned until the foreign service was almost stripped. Thousands of less prominent Cubans found ways to leave their homeland for exile. Most of them had the same complaint: Communist terrorism was enveloping Cuba. The appearance of Russian submarines in the Caribbean gave oblique support to this theory, as did the Marxist tone of an abusive campaign against the United States. A revival of political trials and executions at this time seemed directed not so much at Batista men as at non-Communist critics of Castro.

By the beginning of 1960 the United States was well aware of disturbing developments in Cuba. Yet President Eisenhower favored a policy of forbearance in the hope that the revolutionary fever would run its course. Though it has been denied, it is very likely that Washington again made indirect offers of economic assistance. Such support was more welcome from other quarters. In February, Deputy Premier Anastas Mikoyan of the Soviet Union made a well-publicized visit to the island, after which a Cuban-Russian trade pact was announced. Later it was known that the Soviet Union promised virtually to underwrite the Cuban revolution, its reward being the creation of a major strategic base for Communism in the New World. Cuba would try to transform its economy by cutting sugar production, diversifying its agriculture on a grand scale, and industrializing. The Communist bloc would send technicians and machinery for the new factories and supplant the United States as Cuba's trading partner. Negotiations with other Communist governments in the following months rounded out the pattern of this bold project. Castro's inexperienced and naive associates mistakenly thought it would be easy to achieve.

In March 1960 Castro denounced the Rio de Janeiro pact of 1947, by which all of the American republics had agreed to unite against a Communist effort directed at any one of them. Shortly thereafter,

President Eisenhower decided that Cuban exiles in the United States should be secretly armed and trained for an invasion of their homeland. In April he wrote to a group of inquiring Chilean students that the United States had at first been heartened by the Cuban revolution but that it had become gravely disillusioned by its denial of human rights. American economic aid, which had been on a very small scale even in Batista's best days, stopped altogether in June. Congress granted an administration request in July to eliminate the sugar quota by which Cuba had enjoyed a preference on the American market since 1934 (and which, as Cubans pointed out, had also benefited American sugar growers and exporters). In anticipation of this measure, Cuba expropriated the major American-owned oil refineries, ostensibly because they had refused to process Russian petroleum on the grounds that it was not legally required of them and that the Russian oil would damage their machinery. It was obvious that the rest of the billion-dollar American investment in Cuba was doomed to confiscation.

All during 1960 evidence accumulated of trouble in Cuba, of business dislocations, labor dissatisfaction, and tyranny. The Catholic bishops issued pastoral letters denouncing radical trends in the government. The presence of increasing numbers of technicians from the Communist bloc countries and the creation of a peoples' militia to replace the army, as well as the state farms and the suppression of the right to strike, seemed ominous to many. So did the persecution of nonleftist professors and the arrest of previously friendly foreign reporters. Yet Castro was still idolized by the mass of the population. It could be fairly admitted that he had improved the status of the Negroes and, for the first time, had enforced rigid standards of personal honesty among government employees. The hotels, luxury resorts, and beaches were now available to the common man. The lower classes thought themselves better off, and probably were, while the middle classes by mid-1960 were scarcely suffering. Massive efforts to reduce illiteracy and to provide technical training pointed to the upgrading of the population's skills.

From the first Castro had shown that his revolution was for export. Efforts to arouse the dictator-ridden lands of the Caribbean excited little genuine disapproval, but when he meddled in more advanced countries alarm spread. Brazil seemed particularly vulnerable, and during its campaign of 1960 politicians made pilgrimages to Havana. After the crisis between the United States and Russia over the U-2 incident, street crowds all over Latin America chanted a slogan popularized by Castro, ¡Cuba sí, yanqui no! At Bogotá in July 1960, the United States announced a Latin American aid program that would later be known as the Alliance for Progress. Cuba refused to adhere to its terms, thus excluding herself from the largess. At a meeting of American foreign ministers at San José, however, only cautious support was manifested for a United States resolution implicitly condemning Communist intervention in the New World. Latin America felt both attraction and repulsion for the Castro revolution, as it did for the Yankee. In the United States, opinion was also divided or uncrystallized in 1960. That it was pointing toward hostility was revealed in the presidential campaign of 1960, when both John F. Kennedy and Richard M. Nixon expressed distaste for the Cuban dictator.

Fidel Castro's fondness for playing the international statesman-hero had its fullest expression in September 1960, when he attended the United Nations General Assembly in New York. Though he appeared on only two occasions at the UN, once to treat the delegates to the longest speech in the organization's history, he had a marvelous time with the public and the journalists. He and Premier Nikita Khrushchev offered an exhibition of friendship and revolutionary comradeship. Castro's delegation reportedly picked chickens in their hotel quarters and otherwise indulged in their cult of filthiness. Perhaps the comic aspect of the visit was the only one that counted, for fundamentals did not change. Most Americans regarded Castro as unbalanced, and he did nothing to disabuse them. When he returned to Cuba he opened relations with Red China and hastened the confiscation of American property. Ambassador Philip Bonsal, who had been snubbed for almost two years, was withdrawn to Washington. In January 1961 President Eisenhower broke relations with Cuba after Castro, in an offensive speech, demanded that the embassy staff of the United States be reduced to eleven persons.

By that time flights from Cuba raised the total of exiles since the revolution to 100,000 out of a population of 6,500,000. Since most of the Batista partisans and major landlords and capitalists had departed earlier, the exodus during 1960 consisted mainly of professional people, shopkeepers, and skilled workers—groups who had been the first to welcome Castro and whose loss Cuba could least afford. The revolutionary government continued to antagonize such classes by stifling freedom, postponing elections, and confiscating their properties. Furthermore, a ministry of labor drew control of the unions from the national confederation, which withered away. Communists took possession of power centers throughout Cuban society with a sure touch that leftists had once attributed to the agents of United States imperialism. All industries and businesses were enveloped under government authority with Che Guevara as chief. Euphoric planning, inexperience, and mismanagement depressed economic conditions severely. These measures, along with tales of terrorism spread by the refugees, convinced the United States government that Castro's regime was ripe for overthrow.

During the early months of 1961 wild vituperation of the outgoing Eisenhower and incoming Kennedy administrations poured out of Havana. One charge, however, was not so wild. For weeks, Cuban spokesmen prophesied an American assault on their island. Defenses were alerted, and Communist fighter aircraft with Cuban pilots trained in Czechoslovakia were on their way. Meanwhile, the squabbling exile groups agreed long enough to create a revolutionary council with José Miró Cardona as its president. It was obvious that there was much coming and going of Cubans between New York, Florida, Louisiana, and Central America. One story, in the *Hispanic American Report*, stated that exiles were being trained in Guatemala under American direction, but it received little attention. It seemed unlikely that the United States would break its policy of nonintervention, if for no other reason than that Russia had openly threatened nuclear war if Cuba were invaded.

It was therefore a surprise to the American public to learn that on April 7, 1961, a landing of 1,200 Cubans had taken place on the marshy south coast around the Bay of Pigs. For three days tension was acute. Then came news of disaster. Gradually, the facts emerged. The United States had armed, trained, and transported the warriors and had lost four of its own airmen in the assault. Castro's forces had quickly contained the beachhead and then captured or killed all the invaders. The island had remained calm, with scarcely a flicker of rebellion. At a late moment President Kennedy had decided not to allow U.S. air forces to destroy Castro's nor to cover the landing. His critics insisted that his decision had caused the failure of the attempt, though this conclusion is doubtful. Kennedy's supporters made much of the fact that the plans had been developed by the Eisenhower administration, with the question of air cover not clearly decided. In rejoinder, it could be recalled that Eisenhower had supervised successful landings in North Africa, Italy, France, and Lebanon. The former president himself had little to say, and the American public rallied behind its new leader.

Castro had much to gloat about, and he did not restrain himself. The United States had been caught breaking its much-touted policy of nonintervention! Castro's hold on the Cuban population was shown to be much stronger than refugees had represented it. Russian support, though it was only verbal, had been heartening. Unofficial Latin American reaction was heavily sympathetic to Cuba, even though their governments helped defeat a Cuban move to have the United Nations condemn the American action. Casually, Castro offered to exchange the prisoners for tractors, only to deride many eminent Americans when they took him seriously. After trying the invaders and finding them all guilty of treason, Castro at length agreed in December 1962 to liberate most of them for a fortune in food and medicine supplied by the United States.

The revolution now proceeded openly as a Marxist affair. Private schools were nationalized and clergymen hostile to the movement were deported. Russian machinery, experts, and war materials were flaunted throughout the island. A single party, the United Party of the Socialist Revolution (PURS), was organized to rule the island Communist-style. Guevara's massive project to industrialize the nation and diversify its agriculture under a central planning board, JUCEPLAN, plunged ahead. In December 1961 Castro stated, "I am a Marxist-Leninist and will be a Marxist-Leninist until the last day of my life." Whether he also said that he had always been one—or whether he really had been regardless of what he said—was disputed by those who heard his words. His commitment was now clear, though his fidelity to Communism or to any other cause might well depend upon tactics and personality factors. Most Latin American governments followed the United States in taking an alarmist view. At Punta del Este, Uruguay, in January 1962, at a meeting of foreign ministers of the American republics, Cuba was expelled from the Organization of American States. But six of the largest countries, with two-thirds of the Latin American population, abstained from the vote.

Reports of Cuba's successes and failures during 1962 conflicted wildly, with all statistics being suspect and conclusions of observers being as contradictory as they had been in the case of Russia during the 1920s, Germany in the 1930s, and China in the 1950s. Guevara afterward made surprisingly candid statements concerning the economic follies of the period, particularly the effort to build factories when there were no raw materials for them to process. Deliveries from Communist countries fell far behind schedule, machines could not be repaired, and the industrialization program faltered badly. The effort to change the axis of the Cuban economy by reducing sugar production was later looked upon as misguided. From 6,800,000 tons in 1961, the crop fell to 4,800,000 in 1962 and 3,800,000 in 1963, with poor weather being only a minor cause of the drop. Shortages and rationing might indicate failure of the economic program. Or perhaps they were preludes to disciplined efforts needed for ultimate success. Many, possibly most, Cubans thought the revolution had benefited them. Yet continuing efforts to escape the island, which brought the total of exiles to 300,000 by 1964, were eloquent suggestions of unrest, particularly since the government made emigration exceedingly risky.

During the summer and early autumn of 1962 shrill charges filled the Cuban press and air that another American effort to dislodge Castro was impending. Innocent of such designs, the Kennedy administration issued denials. Senator Kenneth Keating and a few others, however, suspected that Cuba was diverting attention from her own transformation into an outright Soviet base. Some information indicated that thousands of Russian soldiers were arriving by ship, and that Russian bombers and intermediate range missiles were about to nest in the island. The American intelligence agencies insisted that the men were technicians and advisers and that only defensive weapons were being supplied. For an unexplained reason, American air photographic reconnaissance between September 5 and October 14 was ineffective. Military intelligence being what it is, there was no inherent reason why information received by a senator—or by anyone else—might not be more accurate and more wisely evaluated than data gained by official agencies. In this case, Senator Keating was correct. Not until October 16 did President Kennedy receive photographic proof that missiles capable of striking many cities in the United States were being installed in Cuba. Then he acted with great decisiveness.

The president explained the peril to the American public and alerted the armed forces for an assault on Cuba. He called upon the Soviet Union to remove its bombers, troops, and missiles, securing the support of the Organization of American States for his demand. For several days the international situation was tense in the extreme, with nuclear war clearly a possibility. And then Premier Khrushchev capitulated. Possibly he won concessions that have not yet been made public. The awful crisis over, it became evident in the following weeks that Castro had lost face but that he had salvaged some dignity by refusing to permit United Nations inspectors to examine the supposedly vacated sites. Furthermore, the withdrawal of Russian weapons and forces was so slow as to kindle suspicions that the danger had not really passed. Yet a general easing of international tension followed, and the United States appeared to have won a considerable psychological victory.

In historical perspective this victory was ironical indeed. For almost two centuries the United States had enjoyed in Cuba a neighbor that was either harmless or friendly to the point of dependence. Now it was gratified that the island was not openly a military base on her doorstep in the hands of her most dangerous enemy. Brave words by recent presidents, of both parties, that Cuba must never become a Communist wedge in the New World were recalled ruefully. By 1965 the United States could only hope that the chief Communist powers would never again attempt to convert the island into a major offensive base.

There were other possibilities. The Castro revolution might run its course and become mellow. If Cubans could retain mastery of it and parry efforts by foreign Communists to take control, as Castro appeared to be doing after the crisis of 1962, the island might in time revert to its historic role as a major sugar producer without, however, so much outside influence. In 1964 there were many indications that the plans to transform its economy had faded and a massive revival of the sugar industry was under way. It was also possible that Castro would succumb to or be replaced by agents of China or Russia— or that he would be overthrown by non-Communist Cubans.

Whatever the hopes and fears of the mid-1960's, the fact was that the Cuban revolution was proceeding toward socialism with no immediate likelihood of being halted. Castro paid two visits to Russia in 1963 and 1964, flaunting Cuba's alignment with that country. His outright commitment to Communism cost him much prestige in Latin America, where every government save that of Mexico broke relations with Cuba. His influence on potentially revolutionary movements in that area also dropped. While the American effort to boycott Cuba economically was only partially successful, the United States accommodated itself easily to the loss of the island as a source of sugar, an outlet for its goods, and a site for investment. Even the tourist traffic readjusted effortlessly to other sunny islands of the Caribbean. The United States and Cuba were going in different directions—politically, economically, and intellectually. If this trend continued, two countries that had been intimate so long might live in a state of continuous hostility, and hundreds of thousands of Cuba's best citizens might be doomed to perpetual exile. Whatever the promise or menace of the future, the history of the Cuban nation would tend to discourage affirmations from any quarter that it was likely to become the paradise that nature had intended.

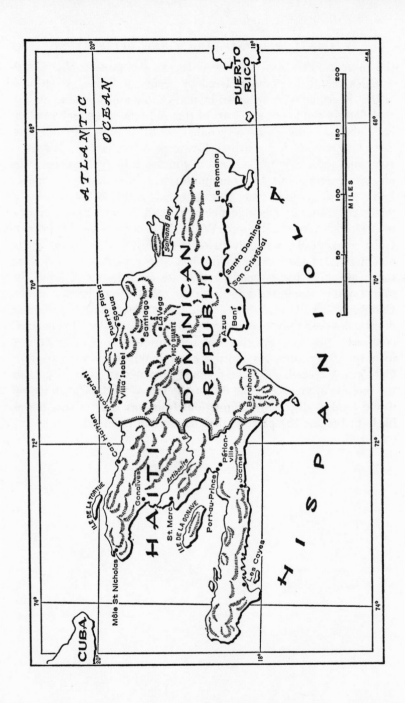

An Anomaly in the Free World

In a different way from Cuba, the republic of Haiti mocks and reproaches the free world, particularly the United States. Presently in the hands of one of the most sinister dictators of its history, the country poses no ideological or strategical threat to anyone. Rather, it exemplifies the failure of its own population—and of outsiders who have intruded upon them—to achieve modern civilization. A beautiful land of 10,714 square miles, with high mountain ranges and stunning vistas, of abundant rainfall and semitropical verdure, most of it is not arable. The part that is supports a bare subsistence for a population of more than 4,000,000, nearly nine-tenths of whom live on small patches of land and use little or no money. It also affords very modest exports of coffee, sisal, and sugar. The people are Negro except for 2 or 3 per cent who are mulatto. Their health has improved markedly in recent years because of medical treatment made available by outsiders, but the average life span is only 35 years. Haitians are reproducing rapidly, far in excess of the country's capacity to feed and educate them. Their folk art, music, and dances are much admired. The patois they speak, derived mainly from French, and the religious practices of voodoo set them apart from their Caribbean neighbors. Except for a small minority of the educated, Haitians generally are not Westernized in their outlook and way of life.

A famous colony of France in the eighteenth century, this land was peopled with Africans forcibly imported to work as slaves on the sugar plantations whose productivity was the marvel of the West Indies. The revolt of the colored population toward the end of that century resulted in the elimination of the white element and the destruction of the sugar industry. Haiti became, however, the second nation in the New World to achieve its independence. Defiant, xenophobic, and isolated, it has been semibarbaric and pitifully poor ever since. Occasional brushes with European powers did little to improve it or to inculcate a desire for greater intimacy. During an occupation from 1915 to 1934 the United States installed some of the rudiments of twentieth-century modernity. For more than two decades thereafter Haiti participated hesitantly in world affairs. And then it turned back on itself, reacting against the outside and the tiny educated class who were Western-oriented. Oddly, this country has never kindled a persistent desire on the part of others, even the Negro community within the United States, to carry through a profound program of aid or uplift. After more than a century and a half of independence, it stands as an anomaly in a world that is urgently seeking material and cultural betterment.

The French Part of Santo Domingo (1492-1789)

It was prophetic that Haiti was the scene of the first known massacre of white men in the New World. Columbus left thirty-nine of his crew from the "Santa María," grounded on the northern coast on Christmas 1492, to organize a base known as Navidad. Nearly a year later he made his way back from Europe, only to find the settlement erased and all of the men killed. As Columbus reconstructed the story, the Spaniards had seized women and goods from the natives and provoked a neighboring potentate. That the "Indians," as he called these natives, were capable of such reaction was a surprise, for those he had encountered in 1492 had seemed kindly and guileless. Most of them members of the Taino group of the Arawak family, they occupied the island of Hispaniola in a state of peace rarely encountered anywhere. Like the natives of Cuba, the Tainos lived in villages of round huts, ate corn and cassava, smoked tobacco, and made baskets, pottery, and polished stone tools. Their religion and morals were primitive; the Spanish found them charming at first, but later so disgusting that any atrocity could be justified. Possibly there were five major monarchs on the entire island, but government was primitive too. On the surface, the Tainos had an island paradise where there was little strife and little labor. Because of their disappearance within forty years after the first contact with Western civilization, they had small effect on the historical evolution of the nations on Hispaniola today, nostalgically as they are regarded.

The western third of Hispaniola, now Haiti, remained almost unpopulated for about a century after the extinction of the Tainos. Spanish explorers examined the area, but except for a few spots on the coast they made no settlements. Even these disappeared in 1605, when the crown ordered the inhabitants to concentrate nearer the capital of the colony, Santo Domingo, in order to reduce smuggling. Wild cattle and hogs overran the region, making food and hides available to sailors who prowled about the Caribbean. In 1631 Englishmen in the employ of a Puritan trading company landed, only to be massacred four years later by the Spanish. In 1639 a nondescript group of Frenchmen, including Huguenot exiles, adventurers, robbers, and pirates, took over the barren island of Tortuga in the north and set up a base. Spaniards drove them off the island in 1654 to the hills of the mainland, with the result that they created more settlements, and they reoccupied Tortuga shortly after. Useful as *flibustiers* or freebooters, pirates, buccaneers, and outlaws of all types found Tortuga and the bays of Haiti during this period, more purposeful men had plans for the area. Colbert, the brilliant minister of Louis XIV, included it in the jurisdiction of the officially-sponsored Compagnie des Indes Occidentales in 1664, and in the following year named an able and experienced governor, Bertrand d'Ogeron, to make it a colony.

D'Ogeron had enough force to compel many of the outlaws to settle down as planters in the fertile valleys of the north, raising tobacco and cacao and cutting mahogany for export. Those who declined to become respectable continued to raid ships or towns in the Spanish and English spheres, often with the governor's connivance. In the long run, d'Ogeron's activities were constructive; a truly productive colony came into being. Women regarded as undesirable in France were imported to become wives of the settlers. Another mark of stability was the immigration of African slaves, mainly from Senegal and other parts of western Africa. This new labor force, which was far more reliable than the unruly whites, made it possible to begin the cultivation of sugarcane on a considerable scale. European vegetables and Asiatic or African importations, such as citrus, mangoes, and breadfruit, provided further sustenance for a growing population, along with the fowl and livestock that had long run wild.

When the monopoly company went bankrupt in 1674, the French crown assumed firm control. A governor-general exercised all military and many other powers, while an intendant handled justice, finances, and various civil affairs. In time a council of colonists was created to advise the governor-general and to serve as a court of appeal. This council tended to press its advice, pretending to register or refuse decrees as *parlements* in France did, but the crown strongly supported its officers in suppressing such tendencies. The administration remained autocratic, though the colonists repeatedly asserted themselves. Governors were usually members of the military aristocracy and flaunted the power of the monarchy with style. For most of the colonial period they were immediately responsible to the minister of marine in Versailles.

The rapid growth of slavery in the French colonial possessions led Colbert to prepare a *Code Noir* in 1685 to regulate the ownership and sale of Negroes, to reduce exploitation, and to assure the continuation of slavery. It contained detailed provisions for the housing and feeding of slaves as well as the protection of their rights. Masters were carefully restricted in their authority and manumission was easy, with *affranchis*, or the freed, allowed all of the rights of other free men. Families were not to be divided, and other safeguards protected the slaves. Humane as the *Code Noir* appeared in many respects, it contained stringent provisions to protect the institution of slavery and prevent rebellions. As was true in other colonial areas, the enforcement of humanitarian laws depended on individual masters, who might be more concerned with their economic stake. Therefore, the code stands as a monument to enlightenment or to hypocrisy, depending on the point of view. Further liberalizing features were introduced in the eighteenth century, but slavery remained hateful, especially as the Negro population came to outnumber the French several times over.

Well-entrenched as France was in western Hispaniola, her title was long void. Wars of the 1680s and 1690s brought garrisons and fleets to the area to make it more French than ever. Though Spain was knocked about the Caribbean mercilessly during those decades, she occasionally dealt hard blows herself, such as razing the principal French town, Cap Français, in 1691. At length, by the Treaty of Ryswick in 1697, Spain acknowledged France's title to the region, which became known as "the French part of Santo Domingo," or Saint-Domingue. Three provinces were marked out. The fertile peninsula of the northwest with the colonial capital, Cap Français, was North Province. West Province was the indented section in the middle, a torrid and often dry area containing the great flat plain, the Cul-de-Sac; its chief city, Port-au-Prince, was not founded until 1749. South Province was the rugged end of the southern peninsula, a backward area little suited to agriculture, with a good port, Les Cayes. By far the most heavily populated of the three was North Province, where the choice lands for raising sugar and coffee were thoroughly cultivated. Because of extensive irrigation works in the valley of the Artibonite, West Province became very productive in the second half of the eighteenth century, while South Province remained largely undeveloped.

From 1697 to 1789 the history of the colony was outwardly calm, with few political or military developments. Its economic growth, however, was nothing less than spectacular, making Saint-Domingue by far the leading sugar-producing area and possibly the richest colony in the world. Since other lands were potentially as productive, the preeminence of this colony must be attributed to the energy and skill of the French. Their importation of slaves eclipsed the volume of this tragic traffic that other nations had. Frenchmen and creoles who so rapidly filled the fertile valleys and irrigated plains with plantations must have been uncommonly efficient. The best in machinery and techniques for grinding sugarcane was installed. Port facilities and roads were extensive, and fortifications, arsenals, and barracks were sufficient to serve the large fleets and garrisons and to deter any serious military threats against the colony. The capital, Cap Français, acquired some beautification and Port-au-Prince grew rapidly, though it retained its tropical squalor. Homes for the possessing classes were generally in the agricultural areas, not in towns. At first merely practical, they became comfortable and often luxurious as the plantations brought in money every year.

The social situation in Saint-Domingue was extremely complicated. Frenchmen occupied the principal posts, the military aristocracy holding itself superior to the civilian *noblesse de la robe* which handled judicial and civil affairs. Creoles were snubbed by the French-born and, to be sure, often were descendants of pirates or low-born adventurers. Those who had become wealthy planters, the *grands blancs*, aspired to govern the colony and resented the officials from metropolitan France. Poor Creoles and white immigrants who had not advanced economically were often called *petits blancs*. As trades-men, artisans, small farmers, or unemployed, they tended to be a restless element. Mulattoes made up the bulk of the *affranchis*, since white fathers often liberated children by Negro mothers, though a few Negroes had also obtained freedom and even owned slaves. By the end of the eighteenth century mulattoes were crowding the *petits blancs* in various occupations, and tension was developing. Segrega-tion of the races in churches and other public places aggravated it, serving to madden the more ambitious mulattoes and to inflate the poor whites.

The Negro population outnumbered the whites and mixed races by seven or eight times by 1789. Nearly all of them were slaves, a majority born in Africa. Naturally, numerous nations and tribes com-posed this element, the oldest groups having originated in West Africa, the later arrivals coming from Angola and the Congo. Their condition varied from plantation to plantation, though the *Code Noir* offered some protection when it was enforced. According to traditions fervently believed by modern Haitians, the slaves were at all times abused in a most inhuman fashion and they seethed with hatred for the whites. Frenchmen and creoles, particularly those who were expelled from the colony after the revolution began, maintained that the slaves were better off than they had been in Africa, that they lived comfortably in the tropical climate with private gardens of their own and only seasonal work to do, and that gaiety rather than hate was the prevailing mood. While discipline must have been severe, there were few massive rebellions. Perhaps the worst scare was in 1757, when François Macandal, a black messiah who claimed to have royal blood, planned an extensive campaign to poison all the whites. He was apprehended and burned alive. Other plots and acts of de-fiance must have been suppressed as fiercely but with less notoriety. *Marons*, or escaped slaves, kept the whites on edge throughout the colonial period. Possibly some circulation of libertarian ideas occurred after hundreds of Haitian Negroes participated in the American Revolution when France aided the insurrectionists.

As smiling a picture of an economic venture as Saint-Domingue offered the French monarchy, it lacked most of the graces of France. The Negroes seldom spoke French, and few were converted to Catholicism. The French spoken by whites and mulattoes was filled with archaic, Norman phrases, words from other European languages, and corruptions from African tongues—becoming the eventual patois "Creole" spoken by most Haitians today. Animistic religious beliefs and practices, possibly originating in Dahomey, with magic and witchcraft as prominent features, spread over most of the Negroid population as Vodun or voodoo developed. Mulattoes were usually European-oriented but lacking in formal culture. *Petits blancs* were often a turbulent, ignorant lot, probably more brutal than the lower classes in France. And the *grands blancs*, for all their extravagant tastes and opulent display, were generally crude and uneducated. Schooling on an institutional scale was unknown in Haiti, though a few boys went to France for education. Even the Catholic clergy was small and comparatively ineffective as a civilizing or humanitarian agency.

In short, Saint-Domingue was a highly profitable business venture for many Frenchmen but a crude and explosive society. According to the census of 1788, perhaps the most reliable statistics ever to come out of Haiti, there were 28,000 whites, 22,000 free colored, and 405,000 Negro slaves. They lived in relative order, but tensions and hatreds were close to the surface. Slavery and tropical conditions debased the moral climate. Also, the presence of great numbers of sailors and soldiers, of officials out to enrich themselves, of business adventurers, and of demoralized officers of an Old Regime about to collapse, further depressed the colony. Nor did the buccaneering tradition and the get-rich-quick ethic serve to create a wholesome environment. Saint-Domingue was a colony in the classical sense, a land to export sugar, coffee, indigo, cotton, and other raw materials to an advanced mother country. Much of its own food was imported. It did not exist for the welfare of its inhabitants but for that of outsiders.

The Second Free Nation in the New World (1789-1915)

Probably the worst massacre in the New World occurred in Haiti during the period of the French Revolution. Initially, the fault was that of the creole *grands blancs*, who tried to take advantage of the convening of the Estates-General in France in 1789 to win control of the colonial government, and thereby began the disintegration of the taut society of Saint-Domingue. They demanded liberty—liberty for themselves to rule the country. Their complaints against the colonial regime were not particularly cogent, for the government was lax, taxation was not burdensome, and the economic monopoly had recently been broken when France opened the colony's ports to foreign ships and concluded commercial treaties with England and the United States. By sending representatives to the Estates-General (later the National Assembly), these creoles inadvertently brought to the attention of French reformers the appalling social conditions of Saint-Domingue. An abolitionist society, the *Amis des Noirs*, poured propaganda into the colony urging liberty and equality, stirring poor whites, mulattoes, and slaves alike. In the early days of the Revolution, in September 1789, the National Assembly gave the *grands blancs* what they wished, decreeing that they could run Saint-Domingue with an assembly of their own. Late in 1790, however, a French-educated mulatto, Vincent Ogé, led a rising in the North and was suppressed, being put to death at the wheel. This barbarous execution aroused the National Assembly to decree, in May 1791, the extension of suffrage to all free persons, including the colored. Strong creole pressure from the colony led to the revocation of this decree in September, just in time to spoil a promising union of white and mulatto forces against the Negroes, who had rebelled a month before.

The rising of the slaves in North Province in August 1791 was the first full-scale rebellion of this nature in the West Indies. Prepared in great secrecy by voodoo leaders who drummed messages all over the plantation area, it caught the authorities by surprise. Probably 100,000 blacks participated, burning homes of the whites, destroying machinery and crops, and torturing, raping, and killing the ruling groups. Cap Français was threatened but for the time being stood firm. As whites, and often mulattoes, rallied, they committed atrocities of their own against the Negro rebels, with the result that the social structure and the economy of the North were ruined. In September 1792, 6,000 French troops arrived. Most of them had been indoctrinated with the Revolution, and most of the commissioners who came with them to represent French authority were Jacobins. The most determined of the commissioners was Sonthonax, who sided with the Negroes and defied both the royalist governor and the creole assembly. Conditions were so desperate for the whites that 10,000 sailed away from Cap Français to the United States. And in August 1793, Sonthonax announced the end of slavery in the colony, an action which the Convention in Paris confirmed in 1794. Saint-Domingue was proclaimed an integral part of the French Republic in 1795.

At war with France and eager to take over her rich colony, Britain and Spain sent large expeditions to Saint-Domingue and allied with whatever forces they could. When news arrived that Spain had, by the Peace of Basle in 1795, agreed to withdraw from the war and cede Santo Domingo to France, the Spanish forces were evacuated. But the British stayed on until 1798, to lose perhaps 40,000 men to yellow fever and in combat. The whites and their mulatto allies who had survived to this point now faced immense danger from experienced Negro armies led by Haiti's greatest man, Pierre-Dominique Toussaint Louverture.

Born into slavery in 1743, Toussaint Louverture had acquired a good education through the aid of his master and had long been a thoughtful student of his people's plight. When the Revolution began, he organized 4,000 Negroes into a private army, which was employed as an ally of the royalists and the Spanish. He switched sides in 1794, murdering his Spanish soldiers in the process, and fought to prevent a colonial restoration. He had exceptional abilities as a military commander. Methodically he defeated the royalists and the British, establishing himself as the principal Negro leader by 1798, when the British withdrew. Toussaint illustrated his statesmanship by negotiating a commercial treaty with Great Britain on that occasion and afterward extending its provisions to the United States. In 1799 he convinced the Directory of the French Republic that he was loyal both to the Revolution and to France, and was named governor-general.

Master of the North, Toussaint proceeded into the West and South to defeat the mulattoes, who had previously removed most of the whites. His subordinate, Jean-Jacques Dessalines, received the mission of liquidating the mulattoes, which he carried out with hideous brutality. In the process, the vast irrigation works of the Cul-de-Sac and the Artibonite were destroyed most of them forever. Meanwhile, another lieutenant, Henri Christophe, began to put back many ex-slaves to producing sugarcane and coffee in the North. Toussaint invited former white residents to return; some of them did. Cunning and treacherous as Toussaint has seemed to many, he was a constructive statesman. He understood the importance of restoring the economy and of maintaining friendly ties with England, France, and the United States. Undisputed ruler of Saint-Domingue, he did not wish to provoke the French. Thus a constitution he issued in 1801 stipulated that his country was part of the French Republic. Also in 1801 he made good the title of France to Spanish Santo Domingo by occupying that colony with his Negro armies. His authority had now reached its peak. Master of the entire island of Hispaniola, adored by his soldiers and the masses, and full of plans for progress, Toussaint pointed to a bright future.

Napoleon, now dictator of France, had regarded Toussaint's achievements sourly. His own plans were to restore the colonial economy and the slavery that supported it. Taking advantage of the brief interlude of peace with Britain permitted by the Treaty of Amiens, he dispatched General Victor Leclerc, his brother-in-law, to Saint-Domingue with possibly the largest expedition ever to sail directly from Europe to America. Napoleon ordered a three-stage reconquest, to open with kindly blandishments and to end with the total restoration of the colonial system. Leclerc arrived in January 1802 and soon overran the island with his troops. Toussaint was removed from command and given a dignified retired status. Presently, most of the French came down with yellow fever. And as suspicions circulated among the Negroes that slavery was to be revived, restlessness became general. Fearful that Toussaint might lead another revolt, Leclerc tricked him into a parley and shipped him to France, where he died a few months later. Leclerc himself died of yellow fever in November. By that time rebellion had flamed all over the land. The sick French forces, even after they received heavy reinforcements, were unable to contend with it. And the renewal of the war with Britain gave the French the alternatives of dying in Saint-Domingue or surrendering to the British; they chose the latter. Late in 1803 the French departed, leaving perhaps 50,000 of their dead comrades on the island.

Toussaint's leadership had fallen to Dessalines, an African-born uneducated warrior who had known the worst ignominy, having been a slave of another Negro. On New Year's Day, 1804, he proclaimed the independence of Haiti (the Indian name, probably denoting *hills*, he chose to give the state), vowing eternal hatred of the white race. This was the first country in Latin America, and the second in the New World, to win its freedom; Haitians have since then boasted that they overthrew the colonial system and defeated Spain, Britain, and France, even the great Napoleon, all by themselves. From now on they wanted no contact with the outside world. When he learned that Napoleon had taken the title of emperor, Dessalines had himself acclaimed as Emperor Jacques I, in October 1804. No titles of nobility were permitted, for Jacques proposed to tower above all. Not much for sure is known of his brief reign, since few literate persons were available to record events, and racism has prompted wildly conflicting estimates. He apparently invited the French planters to return, only to exterminate them with great cruelty. He ordered all Haitians to become either soldiers or laborers and enforced his will with a savage disregard for human decency. Like Toussaint, he tried to suppress voodoo. When an uprising of mulattoes occurred in the South, Jacques headed toward the area, only to be ambushed and barbarously killed, in October 1806.

Henri Christophe was now the leading figure. A constitutional assembly met in December 1806 and named him president. Annoyed because the office had fewer powers than he desired, Christophe spurned it and called another assembly in the North, which made him all-powerful president for life. In South Province and the southern part of West Province, a mulatto group rallied around Alexandre Pétion and elected him to the weakened presidency declined by Christophe. Hence there were now two Haitis and two presidents. After inconclusive fighting, a stalemate was accepted in 1810.

The two men were very different, and so were their policies. Christophe was a Negro born in one of the British Caribbean islands and a onetime slave. Without formal education, he nevertheless had a marvelous memory and great skill in picking the brains of men who were more knowledgeable than he. Violent and cruel, he was also handsome and, when he chose to be, personable. Pétion had a French father and a Negro mother and had been educated in Paris. Having fought at first with the mulattoes on the royalist side, he had fled to France and returned with Leclerc, and then shifted to the patriot cause. Kind, tolerant, and mild, he personified the gentler virtues and lacked Christophe's furious drive.

Christophe took the crown as King Henri I in 1811, after Pétion had been reelected president in the southern part. This elevation called for the erection in a short time of a cathedral for the coronation at Cap Haïtien (formerly Cap Français) and the creation of a huge nobility. Court etiquette and monarchical splendor were designed to exalt his person in the style of Louis XIV. Also an admirer of Frederick the Great, the king used Prussian drill for his troops and constructed a majestic palace named Sans Souci. Using perhaps 200,-000 laborers, he undertook to build a magnificent citadel to protect his kingdom from Napoleon, but it was never finished. A *Code Henri*, devised by some of the experts the monarch employed, gave his realm modern laws, and Henri set up a few schools, a theater, and a newspaper. He insisted that his subjects wear shoes in the capital and that they look their best. He also demanded that they work. Restoring many of the plantations, some of which went to the new aristocracy and others to the state, he compelled the population to labor, often riding about the country with a whip to see that his subjects obeyed. Enough was produced to provide funds for the state and to feed the people. Yet the output was only a small fraction of what it had been in French days, and Henri's methods caused much grumbling. In August 1820 he was partially paralyzed by a stroke. A rebellion promptly broke out, and when, in October, he realized that it was succeeding, Henri I put a silver bullet through his head.

Meanwhile, Pétion's milder rule in the southern half, with its capital at Port-au-Prince, was based on turning land over to small, free farmers, though some mulattoes were allowed to acquire plantations. Pétion also permitted voodoo to flourish. He started a secondary school in the capital and probably intended to build a system of public education. His concern for Negro freedom led him to support

Simón Bolívar in the independence movement in South America in exchange for the Liberator's promise to free the slaves. Although Pétion strengthened the presidency and had himself made president for life in 1816, he was far from being a despot when he died, in 1818. Haitians honor him for his kindness and idealism, yet they tend to regard Christophe as a greater figure because of his efforts to restore the economy.

Jean-Pierre Boyer, a mulatto who was head of the presidential guard, dictated his own election as president for life following the death of Pétion. Soon after the suicide of Henri Christophe, he rallied the northern half of Haiti to his regime. And in 1821, when the hapless creoles of Santo Domingo revolted against Spain and tried to join Bolívar, Boyer led troops into that ancient colony. Early in 1822 it was forced to accept union with Haiti. Little effort was made to strengthen the economy. The only Negro republic in the world, it mocked those who advocated freedom for colonies; "Haitianization" became an opprobrious term in other countries. The population probably enjoyed lives of peace, freedom, and idleness, not caring if the world disdained them. Voodoo flourished, almost replacing the traces of Catholicism left from colonial times, and Rome had no influence on the remaining Catholics. The patois of French, African languages, and sprinkling of English, Spanish, and Dutch words continued to evolve. Having almost no contacts with the outside world and no immigration, Haiti at least developed something of a culture of its own. There was reason to shun the great powers. The United States, England, and Spain might have been tempted to take over the island. Louis XVIII tried to restore the French colony. Charles X, in 1825, sent a large expedition to Port-au-Prince to compel Haiti to promise payment of 150 million francs to indemnify dispossessed Frenchmen, in exchange for which he recognized Haiti's independence. Later, in 1838, Louis Philippe cut the indemnity to 60 million francs, which was far more than the little country could pay for many years.

Boyer was no megalomaniac or brute, but he was dictatorial and cranky. His long rule, from 1818 to 1843, was characterized by disguised tyranny, spasms of violent suppression, and drift. Himself a man of education, he did almost nothing to extend public instruction. While he issued laws based on the *Code Napoléon* and laid out territorial units similar to those in France, he neglected to build an administrative system of probity or efficiency. Economic conditions scarcely improved at all; the sugar mills and irrigation systems remained in ruins. The only article of export that produced significant foreign exchange was coffee, usually picked from wild trees by women and shipped to France or Belgium. Subsistence agriculture on small units in the fertile spots, along with livestock and fowl, provided food for the masses. Gradually, woods were torn up to expand the farming area, and much of Haiti's soil washed away. Only a few foreign merchants risked their capital by starting shops, and they were likely to fail. In fine, Boyer's regime, the longest in Haitian history, was one of slumber and neglect. If any group improved its position, it was the mulattoes, who were coming to style themselves the *élite* and who tried to maintain ties to French culture and Catholicism.

By 1843 Boyer had accumulated many enemies through his abuse of power. He was also in difficulties because of the French indemnity and an earthquake which damaged much of the country in 1842. A sudden rebellion at Praslin sent him into exile. Worse was to follow. A mulatto officer replaced Boyer, only to face an independence movement by the long-suffering Dominicans. Failing to suppress them, the new president was overthrown. The truncated nation, roughly the Haiti of present times, was unable to govern itself. Two octogenarian Negro generals, both illiterate, were made presidents as fronts for the *élite*, each to serve only a short time. A third aged black president died after a year. In 1847 the *élite* made the mistake of naming a brutish young Negro, Faustin Soulouque, who appeared to be a naive and agreeable officer, president of the republic.

Within two years Soulouque learned enough about men and power to overthrow his mulatto patrons and to have himself proclaimed emperor as Faustin I. A costly coronation, a huge nobility, and extravagant monarchical trappings exhausted the paltry income of the state while delighting the black masses. Mulattoes were intimidated, and foreigners had to behave with abject reverence in the imperial presence. Faustin's posturing caused much merriment abroad, reinforcing an image of Haiti as an absurd land. Nothing good can be credited to the ten years of the sham empire except, possibly, public entertainment. In the most cherished goal the emperor had set for himself, the reconquest of Santo Domingo, he failed in spite of much bluster and several invasions. In 1859 the empire abruptly collapsed before a military uprising.

Fabre Geffrard, a mulatto general, seized control of the state and ruled it for eight years, 1859-67. Outwardly gentle and cultured, he handled national affairs more competently than any previous leader. The American Civil War gave him a chance to stimulate cotton-raising in Haiti and to build gins. He sought to lure American Negroes as immigrants, and in 1864 he won recognition by the United States. One of his most far-reaching actions was a concordat in 1860 with the Holy See, by which Rome again asserted control over Haitian Catholics and dispatched clergy to bring them back to orthodoxy. In time, both the Catholic and Protestant missionaries made some inroads into voodoo dominance and established a few schools. Geffrard, himself full of intellectual pretensions but wise, began to send selected youths abroad on scholarships. His aid to education and his vision of a Europeanized Haiti made Geffrard one of the most respected of the nation's rulers. In 1867 his guard betrayed him, turning its guns on the presidential palace, and he fled.

From Geffrard's fall until the American occupation of 1915, Haiti's political life was squalid and almost devoid of coherence. No real issues or ideals stood out. Two political parties had an uncertain continuity, the Liberals and the Nationals, with the former representing the mulattoes and the latter inclined to favor Negroes, but both were essentially instruments of the *élite*. All presidents but one during this period were army officers. Most of them were acclaimed by cowed members of successive congresses following military skirmishes and street riots. It became a practice among politicians to recruit *cacos*, primitive mountaineers from the north, and lead them into Port-au-Prince to overthrow one president and install another. With few exceptions, the *élite* pulled the wires but saw to it that black presidents were in office, thus blunting the antipathy that an obvious flaunting of oligarchy might have created among the Negroes. As time went on, moneyed persons advanced funds for revolutions in the expectation that quick repayment would be forthcoming once they succeeded. There was little purpose in seeking to strengthen or perpetuate a government afterward. Revolutions themselves were a form of money-making. Large loans floated abroad, particularly in 1875 and 1896, the carefree issue of paper money and government bonds, and the use of a national bank established in 1880 to finance such adventures made easy money plentiful for those who could play the game. The republic really had little money, receiving revenues only from the taxation of coffee exports and from swindling foreign investors. And its funds were used for political purposes, not to develop Haiti.

During this long period few public figures stood out for any reason. One who did was Louis-Felicité Lysius Saloman, a Negro who had long lived in Europe. President from 1879 to 1888, he finally liquidated the French indemnity and provided some internal order. Hoping to increase production, he further subdivided the countryside among peasants, but since they raised gardenstuffs and chickens for their own consumption, the national economy was scarcely strengthened. He made, as other rulers had, a half-hearted effort to restore forced labor. This purpose also was defeated, since women performed almost all of the work, often in cooperative labor bees known as *coumbites*, and the men did not care to change the system. Another famous president was Florvil Hyppolite, also a Negro, who served from 1889 to 1896. His renown rests on the dubious project to lease a naval base at Mole St. Nicholas to the United States and on the lavish sale of bonds to Europeans for public works in Haiti that were seldom started and never completed. By 1900, Haiti remained almost as primitive as it had been a century before. Foreign scholars lamented the pitiful decline in its prosperity since French colonial days.

Conditions degenerated further early in the twentieth century, with presidents coming and going at a faster rate. Aged and illiterate rulers issued paper money and bonds, provoked foreigners by failing to meet payments, and were oblivious of their duties. One president was killed when the national palace mysteriously exploded. Another probably died of poison. Social conditions remained primitive and the nation's reputation was bad. Haiti, the second country in the New World to become independent, after a century of freedom ranked last in civilization.

The Impact of the United States (1915-1934)

By not permitting foreigners to own property, Haiti had avoided some types of evils while denying herself many technological and financial advantages. Nonetheless, the foreigner intruded. France claimed the spiritual allegiance of the *élite*, and Frenchmen bought most of Haiti's coffee exports and bonds. German residents were prominent in a few business firms and in public utilities and dabbled in Haitian politics at times. Although the United States had only a minute financial stake in the country, the Yankee was the foreigner who intervened. And he did so under a president who cannot be charged seriously with susceptibility to Wall Street pressures. By mid-1914, Woodrow Wilson was convinced that the Roosevelt Corollary to the Monroe Doctrine needed to be employed to prevent Haiti from provoking French and German creditors by continual defaulting. Both France and Germany made known their determination to share in any arrangement that Wilson made, but by August these powers were absorbed in other matters. Wilson waited for a time, offering advice to successive Haitian governments and keeping an American flotilla in nearby waters.

Late in 1914 a revolution installed a Haitian president who violated previous agreements with foreign creditors by severing the connection of the government and the national bank. He resisted American efforts to regularize matters and fell to a *caco* revolt in February 1915. The newest president, Vilbrun Guillaume Sam, negotiated with the Americans but was suddenly overthrown late in July. As a parting gesture before he took refuge in the French legation, Sam ordered the massacre of political prisoners. Probably 167 persons were butchered. In revenge, Haitians invaded the legation and dragged the fallen president out, literally tearing him limb from limb. This violation of diplomatic immunity provided President Wilson with the excuse he required to order the landing of American forces, supposedly to prevent French retaliation. Long mentally committed to the idea that American intervention was necessary to provide Haiti with a stable government that would meet its international obligations, Wilson now had another motive: the warring European powers must not install themselves in a strategically important location.

On July 28, 1915, American sailors and marines took over Port-au-Prince and shortly thereafter extended their control over the rest of the republic. The Haitian congress, protected from local mobs by American servicemen, elected as president Sudre Dartiguenave, the first mulatto and southerner to hold office for a generation. The election was apparently a free choice, with 94 of the 140 congressmen voting for Dartiguenave. Now the United States presented the new government with a treaty which placed Haiti's finances, constabulary, sanitation, and public works under American control for ten years. After months of protests, which the Americans halted by cutting off funds to the government, Haiti ratified the treaty in 1916 and, as it happened, renewed it for another ten years in 1926. Americans took over, using Haitian ministers they had selected as fronts. Revenues went straight to the national bank, where American officials divided them among creditors and various government departments and, for a time, paid Haitian public employees directly.

Since one of the main purposes of the intervention was to provide a firm government, the United States in 1917 presented a constitution, of which Assistant Secretary of the Navy Franklin D. Roosevelt claimed to be the author, to the Haitian congress. The congress had already displayed a spirit of independence by refusing to declare war on Germany. Now it rejected the constitution. Consequently, the Americans dismissed the body and announced a popular plebiscite to ratify the document. Free public entertainment and feasts provided by the Americans with Haitian funds presumably made the constitution acceptable to the masses, who voted 98,225 to 768 to accept it. Critics maintained that educated Haitians, who were the keenest opponents of the occupation, did not vote at all. The constitution went into effect in 1918, but elections were not held, and congress was not reconvened. Instead, an increasingly uncomfortable President Dartiguenave and an appointed Council of State served as puppets for American naval officers who ran the country. Washington paid little attention to these officers or to events in the occupied republic.

In two respects the Constitution of 1918 represented departures from national traditions. In one, permission for foreigners to own property, Haitian patriots discerned evil intents, though few aliens cared to purchase land in the country. The other made the constabulary or *gendarmerie* the only legal armed force. Slowly organized by American officers, this body took shape as a praetorian guard that later played a large role in dictating policies and presidents. Early in its career it provoked a serious revolt when the American commanders had the unhappy inspiration to put Haitian rustics to work building roads and revived the *corvée*, or labor draft, which had rarely been used since the days of Henri Christophe. A *caco* leader named Charlemagne Peralte raised perhaps 20,000 rural Haitians in rebellion in 1919-20, taking over much of the northern mountain country and threatening Port-au-Prince twice. Since the *gendarmerie* was unable to deal with them, the U.S. Marines were called in, and the rebellion was crushed and Peralte killed. Many atrocities were charged to the American force. Perhaps 2,250 Haitians lost their lives.

By the end of the Wilson administration in 1921, there was much reason for a depressing appraisal of the intervention. The country was more orderly than it had been in 1915, but the recent revolt had cost more lives than most previous civil wars. Constitutional government was not really in effect. Not until 1919, after several false starts, was the currency sound. No one would yet loan Haiti the funds she needed for a multiplicity of projects. It was embarrassing that the defaulted French bonds, which had loomed large as a justification for the intervention, were still unsatisfied. Few public works had been completed, the only notable one being an automobile road from Port-au-Prince to Cap Haïtien. There was still no public education system. Most alarming was the mounting national feeling among Haitians. Even illiterate peasants cherished a belligerent patriotism and xenophobia; to them the Americans were invaders, kindly in many ways but mostly members of the dreaded white race. The *élite* pretended to a Gallic disdain for American crudeness and bitterly resented being deprived of public offices which they had largely monopolized for a century.

During the presidential campaign of 1920, the Republicans had not neglected the issue of the Haitian occupation. In 1922 President Harding improved matters by centralizing American control in a tactful high commissioner, General John H. Russell, and furthering welfare programs. Since President Dartiguenave had grown very restive as a puppet, he was replaced at American bidding by another gentlemanly mulatto, Louis Borno. Soon it was possible to float a loan of $40 million in the United States and to lighten the controls. A railroad long under construction—one cause of the financial confusion before 1915—was finally completed, linking Port-au-Prince to Desarmes. About a thousand miles of roads suitable for automobiles, all that Haiti has ever had, were built. Fiscal stability helped commerce, which rose slowly, with coffee sales to France continuing to comprise most of the exports. Haiti's return to the world community spelled tourists, motion pictures, a few automobiles and trucks, and radios. Under American sponsorship electrical power systems, pure water supplies, and telephone service came into being. Twelve hospitals and more than a hundred rural clinics were built, and vigorous efforts to exterminate mosquitoes and to vaccinate the population reduced the death rate. Lighthouses, wharves, and public buildings brought touches of modernity to the isolated republic. Public education received some impetus as teachers were trained and a few schools were started. Some effort was made to teach farmers scientific agricultural methods. Finally, the *gendarmerie* came into its own both as an instrument for keeping internal peace and for educating Haitian recruits. The Marines were reduced to a half-brigade of about 500 Americans.

Whatever the legal and moral objections to the occupation, it had brought Haiti to the threshold of the modern world. The American impact had stimulated the country without altering its basic structure. In retrospect, it seems curious that Washington and even beneficent and Negro organizations in the United States took so little interest in Haiti, but the rationale of the 1920s did not include massive undertakings to raise the level of undeveloped lands. After the depression of 1929 cut off the modest income from coffee sales and tourism, nationalist agitation reached the point of rebellion. President Hoover sent a commission which made a hasty survey of the situation and recommended withdrawal. Regarding the occupation as a "mess" inherited from the Democrats, Hoover was eager to comply. President Borno, who had maintained a disguised dictatorship in partnership with General Russell, was prevailed upon to call the long-delayed elections, but he disconcerted the political-minded by indicating his intention to continue as president. A serious threat of revolt changed his mind and caused him to resign. The elections of 1930, which were carried out honestly, gave Haiti an assembly, which in turn chose a president, Sténio Vincent. The administration was "Haitianized" and the *gendarmerie* became the *Garde d'Haiti*, a proud body of fewer than 3,000 members and, unusual for Latin America, the proper proportion of officers and enlisted men. It was still difficult to satisfy Haitian nationalism and American insistence on fiscal controls, and negotiations dragged on until 1934, when President Franklin D.

Roosevelt concluded an executive agreement by which the Americans withdrew entirely except for very restricted supervision of the customs.

Haiti Free but Uneasy in the Modern World (1934-1965)

Sténio Vincent remained president until 1941, being reelected in 1935 for a term that was extended from four to six years by questionable means. An educated mulatto, he favored the *élite*, that minute group who did not work with their hands and who by now were likely to marry, wear shoes, speak good French, and profess Catholicism. His regime was authoritarian to the point of dictatorship, and stable enough to permit a modest economic growth even during the depression. During that troubled decade Haiti may have been fortunate in being so isolated and backward that the totalitarians largely left it alone. Her only serious clash with the outside world was the occasion in October 1937 when Dictator Trujillo massacred perhaps 10,000 Haitians who had crossed into the Dominican Republic seeking work. Even this atrocity did not particularly worsen Dominican-Haitian relations, since they had long been as bad as possible. Trujillo later paid two visits to Haiti and was well received. The beginning of World War II all but ended Haiti's long-standing coffee market in France, but a shift to the United States eased the situation.

When Vincent sought to have himself reelected in 1941, street riots changed his plans. The Haitian assembly, as always, chose the new president, a dark mulatto named Élie Lescot. An affable and suave leader, he visited Washington during the war and strove to be a Good Neighbor. Coffee sales to the United States burgeoned, and sisal became an important Haitian export because the Philippine supply was not available. After the war it continued to find markets, constituting Haiti's second export. The Americans used bases in Haiti during the war and improved roads, airports, and docks while finding means to stimulate education and hospital-building. One American undertaking proved a colossal failure, the effort to build a large rubber industry in Haiti. After thousands of Haitians had been resettled, the project collapsed because of the end of the war and the need for raw rubber. The University of Haiti was created in 1944 and other developments were promising, but inflation, postwar dislocations, and his efforts to discourage voodoo made President Lescot unpopular. In the unhappy tradition of Haitian rulers he had extended his term in 1944 for seven years, only to encounter mounting resentment. It was believed, perhaps unfairly, that he had the support of Dictator Trujillo and that the United States was growing cool to him. In January 1946 the *Garde* unceremoniously deposed him.

After fresh elections, the new assembly chose the first Negro president since 1915, Dumarsais Estimé. A new constitution restored the traditional ban on foreign ownership of property and, for the first time, gave labor the right to organize. Soon, the first income tax was imposed. It was obvious that Haiti was in ferment, feeling the effects of black nationalism and of leveling social ideas that had long stirred the rest of the world. A small socialist movement took shape. Among other developments, Negroes were now joining the *élite* as they became educated and more prosperous. Some observers thought there were now two such groups, others that the *élite* was simply being forced to expand. Tension between the blacks and the mulattoes, the *bruns* and the *jaunes*, appeared to be growing, both on class and racial lines. It was felt worst in the *Garde*, which became the *Armée d'Haiti* in 1949 and was more and more a vehicle of the Negroes.

The health of Haiti's population had long seemed hopelessly bad, despite the sanitary and medical improvements of the American occupation and, later, of the Rockefeller Foundation and other agencies. In 1946 a United States sanitary mission undertook to eradicate the worst affliction, yaws, which claimed four-fifths of the population. The disease was easily controlled by penicillin and cleanliness, thus making it possible for this mission, with the aid of the Haitian government and the United Nations, to treat 2,000,000 persons. Yaws practically disappeared, and thoroughgoing campaigns against tuberculosis, hookworm, malaria, typhoid, and other killers greatly reduced the death rate. Accordingly, the population expanded so rapidly that medical resources and food supplies could not keep pace. Haiti remained the poorest country in the New World.

Estimé sponsored a world's fair in 1949 to celebrate the 200th anniversary of the founding of Port-au-Prince, a project that involved the destruction of some of the worst slums of the capital and, he hoped, the initiation of an enduring tourist boom. Indeed the exposition brought many visitors to Haiti and was a major step in the elevation of its popular and primitive art in the esteem of the outside world.

Yet it failed to justify itself financially. This circumstance and the continuing hopelessness of the country's economic prospects alienated the *élite*. In May 1950 congress refused to reelect Estimé, with the result that he called in Negro mobs to wreck its chambers. After fearful riots, the army stepped in and removed the president.

Clearly in command of the situation was the army's commander, Colonel Paul Magloire, a handsome, educated Negro with an appealing personality. Civilized and able, he aroused no basic fears among the mulattoes, and he was almost an idol to the Negroes. It seemed possible that he could gratify the *brun* element without oppressing the *jaune*. Magloire announced that he would accept the presidency only in a popular election, not by the usual congressional acclamation. His campaign was a veritable festival, with free motion pictures, and food and rum being distributed among the people. He won 151,000 votes to 2,000 for an almost anonymous opponent. Taking office with such promise early in 1951, he soon justified the hopes of his supporters as a dynamic, constructive figure, and quickly won the approval of foreigners as one of the most respected leaders in Latin America. He governed with style, relying on popularity rather than fear to dominate the nation. His personal majesty and royal ways endeared him to the masses; the *élite* admired him for his policies. Haiti during his term was one of the freest lands in the tropics, her intellectuals participating in the dialogues that stimulated their kind everywhere, her politicians voluble and vibrant.

Magloire identified the national goals that every responsible student of affairs knew were imperative for Haiti: improved health, education, industrialization, modernization, and productivity. He swept aside the historic reluctance to seek foreign help in achieving them; obviously Haiti needed all the help it could have. American aid was encouraged, the most notable example being a plan for damming the Artibonite River in a gigantic irrigation and electrical power project. Public education was stimulated by a resolution of a conflict between those who favored using the patois instead of French, and American progressive instead of classical methods, in the schools. The decision was to reserve French and the classics only for the advanced grades. Gradually, the administration lost its drive. The problems were too overwhelming, and discouragement came too easily. As the years passed, Magloire's image of benevolence and ability faded. Stories of graft and cynical practices belied the supposed rush to reach splendid goals. Magloire somehow lost control of the army without realizing it until a late hour. He announced that he would not even complete his term, but then held on to his office as though he planned a coup. In December 1956 a general strike and a swift move by the army sent him into exile, to the surprise and dismay of most friendly foreign observers.

A most dreary series of events followed. An army junta assumed control and named two provisional presidents in succession. Damaging accusations against the Magloire regime for peculation and neglect disenchanted many Haitians who had begun to hope. An election of acceptable honesty in September 1957 brought a country physician, Dr. François Duvalier, a Negro known as "Papa Doc," into the presidency. On the surface, he seemed a dull nonentity to head a lackluster government. Unfortunately, Duvalier displayed a most formidable ability in building a personal political machine. Purges removed army leaders, a militia challenged the praetorian role of the *Armée d'Haiti*, and a very skilled secret police, possibly coached by that of Trujillo of the Dominican Republic, introduced a terrorism that Haitians had seldom experienced in recent years. A gang of ruffians known as *Tonton Macoute* murdered or beat citizens who complained. It became clear that Duvalier was a Negro fanatic and that his prime objective was to humble, or even exterminate, the mulattoes. The old *élite* was intimidated so brutally that many left the country, depriving Haiti of doctors and other men with skills so badly needed. When students rioted in protest, Duvalier closed the university and most schools. The clergy loomed as a potential opponent, and so an archbishop, two bishops, and dozens of priests, many of them of French nationality, were deported. Labor unions, which had only begun to function in recent years, were deprived of independence. Conspiracies and demonstrations did nothing to change Duvalier's grim course. His power even survived a period of incapacity brought on by a heart attack. His steady successes gave him an aura of magical power, a belief already well established because of his voodoo practices. The masses held him in awe more and more, while the *élite* remained in stricken silence.

Duvalier ignored evidence of foreign disapproval, even the reduction of military aid and the very sharp drop in tourism and exports.

In 1961 he presented a slate of names for a new congress, which of course was approved by the electorate. Then he announced his own reelection by virtue of that vote, for a term to begin when his present one ended two years later. The American ambassador was withdrawn and aid virtually cut off. Yet in 1963 Duvalier, more powerful than ever, proclaimed a dictatorship openly, declaring that he was an exceptional man of the type that appears only once in a century. In 1964 a rigged plebiscite made him president for life. Hundreds of thousands of rustic Haitians came to the capital to applaud this elevation. There was even talk of Duvalier's being given the title of emperor. Rebuffed by the United States and the post-Trujillo government of the Dominican Republic, he made overtures to Castro, who had sent an expedition to overthrow him in 1959, and to other Communists. With the country in a more hopeless position economically than ever but abjectly obedient to him, Duvalier appeared a demon scientist. Mad tyrants Haiti has known before. By ignoring public affairs its population has survived and increased generation after generation, changing its ways but little. These ways might spell happiness in some respects, but not according to Western ideals of progress.

THE DOMINICAN REPUBLIC

A Gentle Land, an Unkind Fate

For most of its history the Spanish colony of Santo Domingo and its successor, the Dominican Republic, has been a passive victim of forces from the outside. The scene of the first large-scale destruction of Indians as a result of European contacts, this country was slowly peopled by Spaniards and Africans during a long colonial period. Outlaws and enemies of Spain repeatedly buffeted the settlements and discouraged their growth. The Age of Revolution did not bring liberation, but invasion and occupation. A long slumber, or nightmare, had to be endured while Haitians ruled the land, smothering its economy and culture and causing many whites to emigrate. Freedom from Haiti has always been precarious; fear of reconquest by the smaller but more heavily populated neighbor has affected Dominican psychology more than any other factor. It led to a brief restoration of Spanish colonialism in 1861-65 and to bids for annexation to the United States. Moreover, the failure of self-government and the conniving of European financial adventurers resulted in American occupation of the republic from 1916 to 1924. If the population, culture, and economic development of the Dominican Republic have come from the outside, so have most of its difficulties.

The country has an area of 18,816 square miles, of which 17 per cent consist of arable lands, 12 per cent of pastures, and 71 per cent of forests. Four mountain chains run roughly east-west over the land, making it very rugged, especially in the western part, where it is also dry. In the east are humid lowlands where most of the people live, and in the north is a rich and beautiful valley known as the Cibao. According to a 1960 estimate, Dominicans number more than 3,000,-

ooo and have been reproducing at an alarming rate for the past three decades. Immigration has been a small factor in this growth. Though no one knows for sure, it is unlikely that more than 15 per cent of the population is fully white and 15 per cent fully Negro, and the Indian strain is exceedingly small. Most Dominicans are mulattoes. There is only one real city, Santo Domingo (known as Ciudad Trujillo from 1936 to 1961), the oldest permanent European settlement in the New World, with 350,000 inhabitants. Nearly a fourth of the population lives there or in other centers large enough to be classified as urban. Mainly as a result of the material growth fostered by the dictatorship of Rafael Leónidas Trujillo (1930-61), a few hundred Dominicans may be regarded as rich, and a modest but influential middle class exists. Industrial workers are comparatively well off in terms of wages and conditions, but national unemployment has recently been appallingly high, sometimes as much as one-third of the labor force. The rural areas were long in a primitive state and have only partially emerged from it. As a result of Trujillo's policies nearly half the agricultural lands are concentrated in holdings of 500 hectares or more. Population mobility, economic growth, and political control are facilitated by the best network of roads in the Caribbean, a heritage of the American occupation and the Trujillo dictatorship.

The long torpor enforced by Trujillo is only slowly being broken. Considerable excitement attended the election of 1962, the first free one since 1924, but hope that social justice and democracy could be attained were perhaps raised too high. The administration of Juan Bosch, the victor, was easily overthrown by the military only seven months after its inauguration, notwithstanding American frowns.

The new government slowly won United States approval and announced elections for 1965. Before these could take place, however, a sudden uprising, probably in behalf of Juan Bosch, produced scenes of death and terror. In late April and May, President Lyndon Johnson ordered American forces to occupy key positions in the republic, nominally to protect the lives of foreigners. This he did without prior consultation with the Organization of American States, whose endorsement, however, was soon forthcoming. Washington made it clear that a major motive behind the occupation was the prevention of a Communist or Castro takeover of the Dominican Republic and adduced evidence that this possibility was a strong one if the rebellion were allowed to run its course.

Liberty and self-expression have been suppressed so long that Dominicans have only dim traditions and frail institutions. Unpleasant surprises and repeated disappointments have conditioned them to expect failure. Yet hope is not entirely absent. The Dominican Republic has a pleasant climate and has been freed of tropical diseases. Its fertile valleys, grazing areas, woodlands, and mines are productive and can be improved. Industrialization has a good start. Although more than half the people are illiterate, the educational establishment has great potential. With luck, this land might enjoy more of the benefits of the modern world while not losing the easy-going ways of a semitropical society.

To the United States this country has posed occasional problems but has never absorbed much attention. Washington was slow to recognize its independence and was not particularly alarmed when Spanish control was restored during the Civil War. Presidents Andrew Johnson, Grant, and Benjamin Harrison were interested in acquiring naval bases or even annexing it, but other elements of the government were not. Theodore Roosevelt enunciated his famous Corollary to the Monroe Doctrine because of the Dominican Republic's chaotic financial involvements with Europe and stretched his constitutional prerogatives by taking over its customhouses in 1905. Woodrow Wilson further stretched them in 1916 by occupying the country and setting up a lackluster naval administration to govern it. Only minor benefits were experienced while the rich and advanced United States ruled. Dramatic transformation of underdeveloped lands was not in vogue until later years. Despite some criticism of the arrogant nature of the American occupation, public opinion in the United States was indifferent.

The "Era of Trujillo" found favor in the United States, thanks partly to the dictator's subsidies and ingenious public relations, until the late 1950s, when its iniquities were finally comprehended. Most Americans were pleased by the liquidation of the regime after the tyrant's assassination in 1961, and U.S. forces hovered conspicuously near the little republic to discourage a Communist takeover. The United States government rejoiced over the accession of Juan Bosch and lamented his fall. While the American public and officialdom wished the Dominicans well, and were willing to assist them, United States policy was based, as it always had been, on the need to keep the Dominican Republic from becoming a threat to American security. Economic interests were not weighty. American investments of $87 million in the land were small compared to those in other Caribbean countries. Commerce, involving $172 million in exports and $132 million in imports during 1962, was important to the Dominican Republic but not to the United States, its chief customer and supplier. In all, the United States has seldom taken an interest in this land except to keep it out of the hands of its rivals. This would certainly appear to be the reason for the American landings of 1965, the consequences of which cannot be assessed at this writing. Meanwhile, the Dominican Republic, the first area in the New World to become part of Western civilization, has consistently remained on the periphery of that community.

The Land Columbus Loved (1494-1800)

When he arrived in America on his second voyage, Columbus established the town of Isabela early in 1494 on the north coast of the island known in English as Hispaniola. The settlement had a sad history. The scene of ugly phases of the clash of cultures between Europeans and Arawak Indians, it also illustrated the failure of the great Discoverer in constructive labors. He was unable to create a viable community of food farms, warehouses, and missions—the base for further explorations in what he thought was the Far East—and he found only modest quantities of gold. Yet his experiences had great effects on the institutional development of the Spanish empire that later expanded over the Americas. Columbus led the first *entrada*, a formal entry into pagan lands to take possession, when he paraded into the Cibao. He defeated the first massive native uprising against the white man, after which he instituted a method of tribute by which the Indians paid their white overlords in treasure or goods. He also introduced the *encomienda*, a system under which natives were parceled out among Spaniards to labor. The pattern of race relations and, to some extent, of government and economic development, that affected Latin America derived from Columbus' efforts. And although he seemed a failure, the base he established really served for the subsequent conquest of richer islands and parts of the mainland. At Columbus' order, the Spanish headquarters were removed in 1496 from Isabela to Santa Domingo, on the south coast, and the colony took its name from the city. The Indian word, "Quisqueya," dropped out of usage as the natives themselves disappeared. Though Dominicans call their country "the land Columbus loved" on the basis of his first reports, he suffered many disappointments there and in 1500 was removed in disgrace.

In 1502 Nicolás de Ovando began a term of seven years as governor of Santo Domingo. A sturdy and profitable colony was soon functioning. Spaniards arrived by the hundreds to establish farms, ranches, and mines. Though the Indians died off at a shocking rate, some demographic redress occurred as African slaves were imported. Sugarcane and the familiar European fruits and vegetables, as well as fowl and livestock, made Santo Domingo a paying enterprise even as its gold was exhausted. Its chief function, however, was to furnish the horses, food, and equipment for invasions of other areas and to provide the conditioning in the tropics that Spaniards required if they were to survive such adventures. As the bolder men left for Cuba, Puerto Rico, Jamaica, Florida, and South America, Santo Domingo was left in the hands of those who were contented to develop plantations and ranches.

Columbus' son Diego arrived in 1509 to serve as governor until his death in 1526, though he spent most of his term in Spain fighting for his family's right to rule the entire "Indies." Diego built a palace in the capital and held court like a lord, but his authority was circumscribed. An *audiencia*, a high judicial body with some executive functions, was created in 1511 and assumed some of Diego's powers. From 1516 to 1520 the colony was ruled by a group of Jeronymite friars as a consequence of Bartolomé de Las Casas' efforts to protect the remaining Indians. After the Columbus family sold its claims to the crown in 1536, Santo Domingo had a series of governors or captain-generals until 1801. Most of them were peninsular Spaniards, as were other officials. Santo Domingo also had an archbishop for most of the period who wielded some authority over the Church in the other islands and on the northern coast of South America. It was the seat of the first university in the New World, that of Santo Tomás, established in 1538. Despite the prestige of the colony as the oldest one,

Santo Domingo sank steadily in importance. The spotlight of destiny shifted to Cuba, and then to Mexico and Peru. The mainland vice-royalties were far more productive and populous; it was to them that the great fleets carried officials and immigrants, with only occasional ships being detached to serve such sleepy backwaters as Santo Domingo. And from the great continental colonies came the bullion so valued in Europe, while Santo Domingo had little to export save modest quantities of hides, wood, sugar, and cotton.

The insular possessions of Spain became strategic liabilities after the mid-sixteenth century, when foreign enemies, pirates, buccaneers, and contrabandists found their innumerable harbors useful as bases to prey on Spanish commerce. As outlaws and revolutionists have repeatedly proved, it has always been impossible to maintain effective patrols in the waters around Hispaniola, and the inhabitants, like those of Cuba, were easily persuaded to exchange hides and food to smugglers for slaves and finished goods. A tradition of deceiving the government was built up in the colony and persisted under the republic; and the authorities themselves often connived with law-breaking. Contraband was by no means the only problem. Pirates often descended on the island for orgies of plunder and rapine. National enemies kept the coastal settlements under perpetual threat and sometimes landed, the most notable instances being the seizures of Santo Domingo by Sir Francis Drake in 1586 and by Admiral William Penn in 1655. The Spaniards were so pressed in the western end of Hispaniola that they withdrew from it early in the seventeenth century, leaving it for outlaws and, eventually, for France to take. Saint-Domingue then flourished in sugar and coffee production and became so heavily populated with Frenchmen and Africans that it greatly surpassed Santo Domingo economically and has ever since held far more people.

Generations passed in what was, for Santo Domingo, a somnolent period. Only toward the end of the eighteenth century did the colony become somewhat invigorated. By 1800 the white population may have been about 40,000, while there were around 60,000 Negro slaves, many of whom had been illegally imported, and perhaps 25,000 free mulattoes. Only two of the towns were large: the capital, Santo Domingo, with its graceful colonial architecture and European ways; and the ranching and agricultural center, Santiago de los Caballeros, a rustic town in the Cibao. The others were mere villages and almost as primitive as the Indian towns Columbus had seen. Plantations for sugar, cotton, and cacao occupied fertile regions in scattered parts of the island, usually not far from the coast. In the center were woodlands and grazing lands, often unclaimed by individual owners. A dull jewel in the Spanish crown, far outshown by the mainland colonies and even by Cuba, Santo Domingo also suffered by comparison with Saint-Domingue, which had only a third its size but four times its population.

Black Oppression (1800-1844)

The Spanish-speaking colonists of Santo Domingo were concerned when they heard of the massive slave uprisings in the French part of the island and when, in 1794, Toussaint Louverture deserted his Spanish sponsors to aid the freed Negroes. Nothing, however, prepared them for the stupefying news that Spain had, by the Treaty of Basle in 1795, ceded their land to France. Appeals to Madrid accomplished nothing, and though the French were unable to occupy the area for the time being, the more far-sighted Spaniards and creoles began to emigrate. Negro unrest, blockades, and piracy added to the demoralization. Late in 1800, Louverture, by now virtual dictator of Saint-Domingue, led his disciplined armies into Santo Domingo and quickly overran it. Soon after he entered the capital, in January 1801, he announced the emancipation of the slaves and the incorporation of the former Spanish colony into his own state, which was nominally part of France. The famous Negro leader was much less fierce than the creoles had feared, but many of them departed. In 1802 Leclerc and his fresh forces from France occupied key parts of the entire island of Hispaniola and reduced it to Napoleon's control. Yellow fever soon carried off most of his men, and himself. While the surviving French were evacuating Haiti, General Louis Ferrand disobeyed orders to leave, and led his forces into Santo Domingo, where he established a government for the Spanish-speaking portion of Hispaniola. In 1805 Ferrand's units and the Spanish elements withstood a frightful Negro invasion from Haiti and restored some order and prosperity to what was now a French colony.

News of Napoleon's overthrow of the Spanish Bourbons in 1808 prompted the Spaniards and Creoles in Santo Domingo to rebel against Ferrand, who committed suicide. In December this group, led by Juan Sánchez Ramírez and given naval support by the British, proclaimed the restoration of Santo Domingo to the Spanish empire. Spanish rule between 1808 and 1821 was so inept that Dominicans now refer to it as the "silly Spain" period. Under the liberal government set up during the absence of Ferdinand VII modern ideas were circulated, only to be harshly suppressed after that monarch returned to the throne in 1814. Ideological confusion was magnified as insurrectionary movements against Spain spread over the mainland during these years and when, in 1820, Ferdinand VII was forced to accept liberalism at the dictation of the Spanish army. Since economic conditions had been desperate since 1795, Dominican creoles had little taste for prolonging Spanish rule, whether liberal or conservative. In November 1821 the lieutenant governor, José Núñez de Cáceres, and various creoles of the capital proclaimed the secession of "Spanish Haiti" and sent an emissary to South America to arrange for its union with Simón Bolívar's republic.

Bolívar was in no position to help the Dominican rebels. In Haiti, however, Jean-Pierre Boyer had recently established a strong government. Shortly he led invading forces into Spanish Haiti and occupied Santo Domingo. The hapless Dominicans put the best face they could on matters in February 1822 by accepting union with Haiti, a tie which they really regarded as a calamity. Indeed it was. For the next twenty-two years they were ruled by Haitian Negroes who envied and suspected them. Emigration of Spanish and creole elements was heavy, plantations reverted to nature, businesses and towns disappeared. The ancient university closed, as the few other schools did, and most churches were left without priests. Only lack of organization on the part of the Haitians kept conditions from being more degrading than they were. Perhaps the only constructive achievements of Boyer's regime were the publication of laws based on the Code Napoléon and the settlement of a few hundred Negroes from the United States in Samaná. Otherwise, the story was one of deterioration in every line of civilized endeavor. It is likely that the population declined; according to some estimates it fell to 60,000, about half the 1800 number.

Uneasy Independence and Spanish Repossession (*1844-1865*)

Juan Pablo Duarte and a few other Spanish-speaking creoles and mulattoes organized a secret society, *La Trinitaria*, in 1838 in the hope of recovering independence and promoting liberalism. Their opportunity came in 1844, after Boyer had been overthrown and Haiti had become disorganized. In February they proclaimed the independence of Santo Domingo. The liberal triumph was short-lived, for the Haitians invaded and were turned back by rustic bands led by caudillos who had little interest in ideology. Presently, the most successful of them, Pedro Santana, took over the capital and exiled Duarte and his allies. This uncouth warrior loved power for its own sake and felt the temptation to make public office profitable for himself. Yet he probably meant well and was, in a deep sense, patriotic. To him, patriotism meant keeping the country out of Haitian hands even if he had to place it under European or United States control in order to do so. Certainly there was little to build on: an illiterate, demoralized population of impoverished mulattoes, no commerce or industry, and only subsistence farming and livestock-raising to support economic life. Memories of gentler days were all but obliterated, and ideals had no meaning except for the few men like Duarte, who were expelled.

Santana was informed enough to issue a constitution for the new nation, now called the Dominican Republic, and to have himself named president. Rural leaders like him raised bands and contested his power, and in 1848 he was bested in a power play and resigned. He restored himself in 1849 as the principal military chieftain when the dreaded Negro tyrant of Haiti, Faustin Soulouque, invaded the Dominican Republic, and he defeated the attempted reconquest. Instead of becoming president again, he allowed an ally, Buenaventura Baez—a mild-mannered gentleman who had acquired some sophistication during a long residence in Europe—to serve for four years in that capacity, while Santana remained head of the military forces. The two leaders were preoccupied with fending off another invasion from Haiti. Nearly all of their efforts went into maintaining enough forces to discourage one and in soliciting support from Spain, France, England, and the United States, none of whom exhibited much sympathy for the republic. Not even requests for the establishment of a protectorate met with enthusiasm.

Baez offended Santana by bringing in foreign clergymen to restore the Church, and Santana offended Baez by usurping his presidential prerogatives. In 1853 Santana took over the presidency and declared his former partner a traitor. There followed renewed efforts to interest foreign powers in establishing a protectorate, but none wanted it badly enough to risk antagonizing the others, with the result that, in 1855, Haiti made another effort at reconquest. Soulouque, now the imperial Faustin I, led 30,000 soldiers into the Dominican Republic, vowing to kill everyone, even the chickens. Again, Pedro Santana turned back the offensive and saved the republic, whereupon he retired from the presidency. In 1856 Baez' supporters managed to recall their leader and make him president. Baez evened the score with his old ally by deporting him. But Santana returned in 1857 and ousted Baez, and soon afterward resumed the presidency. In the see-saw politics of these two figures there was little that was edifying. Neither seriously represented any ideal, cause, or program. The revenues of the little republic amounted to scarcely a million dollars a year, but they were sufficient to tempt caudillos to seize public office. And opportunities to take land and livestock or to issue paper money were also attractive.

Not until the end of 1860, when the United States began to break up before an impending civil war, was a foreign power willing to assume control of the Dominicans. Spain was the only taker, and her price was high: nothing less than the restoration of the land as an overseas province of the monarchy. By March 1861 Santana was able to announce that Isabel II had consented to reign over the ancient colony established by Isabel the Catholic provided there was unanimous sentiment on the part of the prospective subjects. It was easy enough for Santana to stimulate, or to issue without authorization, requests from the various towns inviting the queen to accept them. Spanish troops arrived in April, and Santana was named captain-general. Hopes were high for a moment. In Madrid, Spanish pride was fired by the repentance of a former colony and the possibility of further successes in America. In Santo Domingo, relief from the Haitian menace, orderly government, redemption of paper money, and prosperity were benefits expected of the new relationship.

As it happened, Spain was scarcely able to manage its own affairs effectively or to rule Cuba and the Philippines, much less expand her responsibilities. Only in redeeming paper currency, an accomplishment that pleased the Dominicans who had sponsored the restoration, did the government of Isabel II justify expectations. Though it is true that Haiti was deterred from undertaking outright invasions, the Haitians feared that France might copy Spain, and they incited the Dominicans as much as they dared. Santana and his supporters had anticipated the creation of numerous government positions for their benefit. Instead, Spain dispatched hundreds of peninsulars to take over the province. Commerce improved little, and new capital did not arrive. Rather, taxes were imposed and business suffered. Furthermore, Spanish clergymen were shocked to find how far the Dominicans had lapsed in authorized practices, even to tolerating Protestant missionaries. Severe measures were taken to correct the situation. Spanish soldiers behaved the way occupying troops usually do and created resentment. In less than a year Santana realized that things were going badly and resigned, possibly in the hope of being recalled with enhanced powers. Instead, he was made a marquis and retired. His successor Rivera typified the haughtiness associated in Latin American minds with Spanish colonialism, and he antagonized the Dominicans by seeking to curb gambling and vice. When he tried to institute a system of forced labor for public projects, he created a spirit of revolt.

The War of the Restoration, as Dominicans call it, began in 1863 and spread rapidly. Already badly crippled by yellow fever, the Spanish army was unable to strike down the rural bands that multiplied in the mountains. Pedro Santana accepted an appeal to serve the crown in suppressing the rebellion, but he soon felt himself downgraded by Spanish officialdom and protested so passionately that he was on the point of being deported. Before this could take place he died, possibly by suicide. By 1864 the Dominican patriots had organized a government and cleared all but the capital and a few ports of the royalists. In Madrid, where there had always been misgivings about the adventure, the anti-imperialists gained the upper hand. It was obvious that the rebellion would be costly to put down and that Santo Domingo held little promise for Spanish profits in any case. Furthermore, the Civil War in the United States was coming to an end, and Washington had indicated its disapproval of the Dominican affair. In an uncharacteristic display of wisdom, the regime of Isabel II decided to liquidate the enterprise. The last Spanish troops left by July 1865.

Failure of Self-Government (1865-1916)

If little good had come of the Spanish occupation, at least the Dominicans had gained some self-confidence and an attachment to freedom that would persist. Otherwise, things were depressingly the same. Santana was gone, but Buenaventura Baez was available to continue the sorry political game. In December 1865 he was president again. A few months later he was ousted by the "Blues," a faction mainly of rural caudillos from the Cibao. Baez returned in 1868 as leader of the "Reds" and managed to stay in power for six years. His chief accomplishment was the notorious Hartmont bond affair, in which a London firm delivered a small amount of money to the Dominican Republic while saddling it with a debt of several times the figure. Baez also intrigued with various promoters and politicians to sell naval bases or special rights to the United States during the Andrew Johnson and Grant administrations. He even tried to have the Dominican Republic annexed to the United States and possibly would have succeeded, for President Grant was enthusiastic, but for opposition in the U.S. Senate led by Charles Sumner, a hero to modern Dominicans. These projects encouraged Grant to keep American naval units in Dominican waters for several years. When they were withdrawn, in 1874, Baez promptly fell from power.

After two years of "Blue" rule, Baez bounded back into the presidency late in 1876 for his sixth and final term, which lasted for almost two years. As always, the gentle-looking Baez misused the republic's paltry revenues and employed illegal means to vex his opponents. The country remained impoverished and backward, ignored by most of the world. A dim sign of improvement appeared during the Cuban Ten Years' War, 1868-78, when a few planters transferred their sugarcane-raising enterprises to the Dominican Republic. Gradually, the industry grew, with foreigners for the most part owning the plantations. Years passed before exports were adequate to provide sufficient revenues and foreign exchange. Occasionally, businessmen established shops or small enterprises in the republic, but few did well enough to encourage emulation.

After Baez' final retirement in 1878, power went to the "Blues," who had a few leaders of patriotism and competence, notably Ulises Espaillat and Gregorio Luperón. The figure who emerged to power, however, was as thoroughgoing a tyrant as the land was to know until Trujillo: Ulises Heureaux, a Negro whom the Dominicans called "Lilís." He was probably not a native Dominican, though he claimed to be, and as a Negro he had to overcome the formidable prejudice that Dominicans bore toward persons blacker than themselves. Resplendent, tall, and noble in bearing, Heureaux had many advantages. He was a fierce warrior, a cunning politician, and an able showman. Proclaimed president in 1882 by one of the handpicked assemblies the Dominicans called congresses, he served a two-year term and then installed a puppet for the next term. In 1886 he returned to the presidency and held it until his murder in 1899. A typical tropical tyrant, he ruled severely, sometimes sadistically and with cruel humor. Probably he was popular; certainly he was respected. For the first time the republic had a master who enforced internal order. Some economic progress was accordingly possible, especially for foreigners who bought up and cultivated land for sugarcane. A few short rail lines were built to expedite the shipment of raw materials to the ports, and a cable, wharves, and telegraph lines offered modest evidence of modernity.

Heureaux made use of the pacified state of his country to borrow money from abroad. The external debt grew tenfold during his regime. The Hartmont bonds were refunded and another loan arranged through a Dutch company, Westendorp, which received the right to place an agent in each customhouse to collect duties as security for the bonds. In 1893 Westendorp sold its rights to an American firm, the San Domingo Improvement Company. The device did not work well, since Heureaux disregarded the company's agents, and there was no way to check contraband. The dictator himself is supposed to have cheated the customs. He also resorted to the traditional way of seeking American money by offering concessions in Samaná Bay, but premature publicity and poor timing spoiled the project. There was enough money to finance Heureaux's extravagant scale of living and to maintain his oppressive political system, but little benefit came to the country. By 1899 the bonds were in default and many foreigners were irate. Heureaux did not have to resolve the situation. He was shot to death by the promising young caudillo, Ramón Cáceres, in July 1899.

For seventeen years, from 1899 to 1916, the Dominican Republic was in a state near anarchy. The main political groups were *horacistas* and *jimenistas*, taking their names from Horacio Vázquez and Juan Isidro Jiménez, respectively; but assorted liberal reformers and rural caudillos of the most primitive type complicated the scene. Despite bombastic patriotic and regenerative slogans, none of the factions stood for any firm purpose. Even after one or the other had seized power, usually by conquering the capital and staging a mock election by a hastily assembled congress, it devoted its efforts to collecting such public funds as there were for private use and trying to prevent its competitor from ousting it. In the countryside, bands of armed men moved about, shifting allegiances and stirring up trouble. The public came to scorn all politicians and to regard national affairs apathetically. Law, order, and administration scarcely existed. Very few schools functioned. Merchants learned not to accumulate large stocks for fear of being raided and looted during political strife; landowners lived in constant tension that their workers would depart for political adventures or flee, that their crops would be burned and their livestock driven away.

By 1904 the Dominican Republic was so far in arrears on its debt payments to foreigners that the United States feared that a European power might go beyond the familiar gunboat diplomacy and acquire bases, a matter of particular concern by then, since the Panama Canal was being built and Cuba and Puerto Rico were in American hands. Furthermore, a recent decision by the new international court at The Hague in the Venezuelan claims case had given priority to nations that employed force in collecting debts. President Theodore Roosevelt was not willing to let the Dominican situation become so bad that European naval powers might be tempted, and so he devised the so-called Roosevelt Corollary to the Monroe Doctrine, by which the United States sought to prevent conditions in the Caribbean that might provoke intervention.

Roosevelt himself did not want an American protectorate over the

Dominicans nor even much involvement in their affairs. Yet their financial plight was truly serious. Of $1.8 million in revenues, $1.7 million were needed to service the bonds. The debts themselves were a welter of confusion arising from scandalous transactions in the past by European bankers and Dominican rulers. Was there really a danger that one or more of the powers would intervene? Roosevelt insisted that there was, and perhaps he was supported by verbal evidence. Diplomatic papers now available do not indicate that intervention was likely. The president acted on his own apprehensions and, to be sure, was requested by the Dominican president, Carlos Morales, to straighten out the debt situation.

In January 1905 an executive agreement between Roosevelt and Morales gave the United States the right to adjust the foreign and internal debts of the Dominican Republic and to determine the validity of the various claims. The Americans took over the customhouses and agreed to give at least 45 per cent of the receipts to the Dominican government, using the remainder to service the debts. Skepticism of Roosevelt's motives and hesitations on many grounds in the U.S. Senate delayed approval of this arrangement in treaty form until 1907, but it operated from 1905. According to the Americans it worked well. The debts, which came to $40 million, were slowly paid off, and the Dominicans received more funds from the 45 per cent share of the customs than they had from the full amount before. Public administration, production, and commerce improved almost from the first; foreign trade more than tripled in the first ten years. Yet the Dominicans cherished a love of liberty that had survived all the years of anarchy and dictatorship, and they chafed at Yankee tutelage. President Morales himself came to resent it. Late in 1905 he revolted against his own administration and lost out entirely. Replacing him was Ramón Cáceres, an *horacista* who had killed the dictator Heureaux.

Cáceres held the presidency for six years, during which the customs treaty functioned well enough to please Washington and the foreign creditors. An acceptable measure of order prevailed, and Cáceres sponsored long-needed public works and showed more respect for constitutional practices than most Caribbean rulers. In November 1911, however, he was assassinated, and the country quickly reverted to confusion and strife. Matters were further complicated by bad relations with Haiti over the location of the boundary. Thanks to American pressure and the conspicuous availability of U.S. Marines, a peaceful if provisional settlement was made. Late in 1912 the United States forced the resignation of President Eladio Victoria by withholding the Dominican share of the customs. His successor was a neutral figure, Archbishop Adolfo Nouel, who was expected to hold the government together in the face of riotous factions. In a matter of weeks, however, the clerical president had a nervous collapse and quit.

By this time, March 1913, President Woodrow Wilson had taken office and appointed as minister to the Dominican Republic and customs receiver men who were later derided as "deserving Democrats." Inexperience and tactlessness on their part worsened a situation that was already chaotic. Rebellion was endemic throughout the little republic, and finances were again snarled. In October 1914 the Americans pressured the Dominicans into holding a general election, which featured the candidacies of the original *horacista* and *jimenista* themselves. Jiménez won by a narrow margin, an outcome that his opponents took with ill grace. He was now old and weak. His war minister, a trouble-maker of many years' experience named Desiderio Arias, set out to overthrow the president. By May 1916 Jiménez was at bay. He pleaded with the United States to rescue him; soon he retracted his request and resigned, leaving the political situation confused beyond comprehension.

Another Occupation (1916-1930)

President Wilson required no further proof that the Dominicans were incapable of self-government. Furthermore, he suspected that German agents were magnifying the troubles of the little republic, and he regarded the recent American takeover of Haiti as a good precedent. Accordingly, he ordered the occupation of the Dominican Republic. This was accomplished quickly and peacefully. Wilson informed the Dominican congress that he would recognize no president who was not sympathetic to the customs controls and a constabulary directed by Americans. The congress objected, but finally it elected a relatively apolitical person as provisional president, Dr. Francisco Henríquez y Carbajal, who was then in Cuba. The new president stoutly resisted the Haitianization of his country at American hands and declined to retreat even after his funds were cut off. After some months of wrangling, and after his own reelection, President Wilson ordered Captain H. S. Knapp of the Navy to take over the Dominican government. On November 29, 1916, Knapp proclaimed the occupation of the country with himself as military governor. The official justification for this action was that the Dominicans had broken the treaty of 1907 by increasing their public debt and that they needed order and reform. Worsening relations between the United States and Germany were, of course, important if not decisive considerations. The Dominican Republic, as well as Haiti and Cuba, could not be permitted the luxury of wallowing in anarchy when war loomed.

Officers of the U.S. Navy and Marines were the virtual rulers of the Dominican Republic from 1916 to 1922, most of them unwilling and not particularly qualified for the task. They took over the ministries and other executive departments, utilizing Dominicans on the lower levels. Congress was disbanded, certain judges were dismissed, and provost courts assumed many judicial functions. While the Marines guarded the country and suppressed guerrilla warfare and what was too loosely called banditry, a constabulary, the *Guardia Nacional*, was slowly organized. One of its most fervent recruits was young Rafael Trujillo. The disarming of the population probably constituted a social gain, though Dominican boys who were accustomed to receiving pistols when they came of age felt aggrieved. Thanks to wartime prosperity and greatly expanded exports of sugar and cacao, revenues were high. These were used to continue the debt payments, to finance the occupation, and for modest public works as well as educational and sanitation enterprises. For the first time roads suitable for automobiles were built, and wagon trails were so improved that economic unity and military movements over the whole republic were feasible. Within two years the student population rose from 18,000 to more than 100,000. Campaigns against mosquitoes, as well as other sanitation projects, greatly improved the health of the Dominicans—and began a formidable population expansion.

Other American activities caused criticism. Tariff regulations were devised to lower the cost of necessaries, but Dominicans charged that the United States was merely trying to unload its goods on them.

Land title decrees, long needed, were said to be designed to facilitate the acquisition by foreigners of plantations and ranches. Censorship went far beyond the legitimate requirements of the war years and actually became tighter after the Armistice. Educated Dominicans complained bitterly about it. One of them, the poet Fabio Fiallo, who was jailed in 1920 for violating the censorship, was idealized as a hero by Latin Americans critical of the United States. American servicemen were accused of brutality, even atrocities, sometimes with good reason, usually not. In any case, they were inclined to sneer at the backwardness and Negroid character of the Dominicans. After the departure of Knapp in 1918 and a general turnover of occupation personnel, conditions apparently became worse. Succeeding American officers were less tactful, and Dominicans were becoming more resentful. By 1920 nationalistic passions were close to the point of rebellion.

During the presidential campaign of 1920 the Wilson administration was harshly criticized by the Republicans for the Dominican occupation. In December, after the Democratic defeat, Wilson announced that the American forces would be rapidly withdrawn. President Warren G. Harding was entirely willing to fulfill this vow, but it proved unexpectedly difficult to arrange details with Dominican leaders, particularly in connection with the fiscal controls and the constabulary. Not until 1922 did the Americans scale down their conditions sufficiently to win Dominican agreement. A provisional government was then formed to hold elections, following which the Americans would evacuate the country except for supervising the customs and debt payments. The election took place in 1924, with the long-time head of the horacistas, Horacio Vázquez, winning. He was inaugurated in July, and the Marines left in September. While the eight-year occupation had brought fiscal order, improvements in education and transportation, modern sanitation, and, usually, internal peace, it had not engaged the sympathies nor fired the imagination of Americans who might have been interested in uplift programs. In comparison to the extensive welfare and developmental projects undertaken after World War II, the Dominican effort was pathetically timid, altogether insufficient to compensate for the ill will created in Latin America and the resentment of the Dominicans toward the United States.

The six years of the Vázquez presidency were quiet and peaceful.

Dominicans enjoyed more liberty than they had ever known, and the new institutions, based on the constitution of 1924, functioned reasonably well. The constabulary became the national police, and then the national army, with Rafael Leónidas Trujillo eventually as its commander. It was clearly effective in keeping order. Slow but continuous economic and technological advances characterized this period, with sugar production being the principal source of prosperity. Foreign investors purchased plantations, ranches, woodlands, and businesses on a small scale. They were far from comprising a major factor in the economy; rather, they were a stimulus. Of course, the republic remained very poor, with most of its people having only enough for subsistence and being as yet largely undisturbed by the revolution of rising expectations. The middle class was small, and perhaps only three families in the country could be considered rich. Political life was not robust; except for a few educated persons, the Dominicans lacked both the experience and the spirit to take public affairs very seriously. President Vázquez asserted that his presidential term should be six years, as an earlier constitution had specified, instead of the four permitted by the constitution of 1924. However, he invoked the newer one in announcing that he would run for reelection, which was forbidden by the earlier constitution. Although Vázquez was old and no longer vigorous, he had considerable prestige, and little opposition greeted his plans.

The Era of Trujillo (1930-1965)

It happened that Rafael Trujillo was now prepared to grasp for the highest office in the land. He had risen rapidly. Born in 1891 of a poor family, his father having been a part-time postal clerk in a small town, Trujillo had joined the constabulary created by the U.S. Marines and eagerly adopted its cult of toughness. Through energy and ability, and probably skill in undermining and trapping his superiors, he had become head of the army. President Vázquez trusted Trujillo. When a seemingly formless rebellion began in the Cibao in February 1930, the president allowed the commander to deal with it as he wished. Trujillo did nothing. Presently, a few hundred rebels walked into Santo Domingo unopposed. Trujillo literally held the fort, the one that dominates the capital, while President Vázquez and his government were evicted. At this point Trujillo recognized the rebel leader as provisional president, according to a prearranged plan, and announced his own candidacy for the presidency in the elections scheduled for May.

Opposition mounted, finding a focus in Federico Velázquez, a respected political figure of much experience. Trujillo made it clear during the campaign that he proposed to overcome his own lack of popularity by having soldiers intimidate his opponents. The sorry display of undemocratic procedures culminated on election day, when Trujillo proclaimed that he had received 95 per cent of the votes. Immediately thereafter, his recent opponents were rounded up and removed from the public scene. The whole affair was distressing to the United States, which had taken pride in the Dominican army born during the occupation. It was obvious that this force was capable of doing more than keeping order.

The advent of Trujillo appeared to be a typical Caribbean power play, proving only that the Dominicans had not yet learned constitutional ways. Yet it was the beginning of one of the most evil and enduring dictatorships in Latin America. Trujillo ruled for the rest of his life, until 1961. He was president from 1930 to 1938 and from 1942 to 1952. Between 1938 and 1942, and after 1952, the tyrant permitted the presidency to be occupied by puppets, notably his insignificant brother Héctor. All of the political parties were combined into one, the Dominican, which glorified its master and won all of the elections. Once, a Trujillista Party was permitted to enter the field, and from 1945 to 1947 Communists were allowed some participation in politics and two other parties named harmless candidates. The experiments with pluralism had little significance; they ended with no visible display of concern. Truth to tell, Rafael Trujillo was immensely popular with most Dominicans and probably could have won free elections, though he never risked any.

Trujillo was 39 when he became president. Information concerning his youth and early career disappeared, so there was no way to support or refute rumors of difficulties, crimes, or setbacks in his rise to power. Instead, a romantic cult made him a demigod. Joaquín Balaguer, later president of the republic, wrote that the Dominican nation was protected by Providence prior to 1930, and afterward by Trujillo. The dictator was clever in destroying persons or papers that revealed too much about him, extravagant in subsidizing those who rewrote history to glorify him. Dominican intellectuals who remained alive and free during his rule had to be panegyrists. Many foreigners honestly admired Trujillo and said so. Others were bribed into lavishing absurd praise. Billboards and newspaper advertisements in the United States hailed his achievements. Somehow, the tyrant had a childish mania to be admired in the United States, even as he privately relished his reputation as a diabolical genius. In exacting encomiums he had no taste or inhibitions. During his first term he prompted congress to name him Generalissimo and Benefactor of the Fatherland. In 1936 the ancient capital Santo Domingo, the oldest city of European origin in the New World, became Ciudad Trujillo. The sign, "God and Trujillo," appeared everywhere, and the period following his inauguration in 1930 was officially designated "The Era of Trujillo." Busts and portraits of the despot were in evidence everywhere, in homes, shops, offices, and all public places.

Rafael Trujillo was tall for a Dominican, martial in bearing, dignified, and rather good-looking. He had immense force, a hypnotic manner that could entrance or terrify others. His air of authority put him in command of any gathering. Although he had little formal education, he looked wise and knowledgeable, and he was blessed with a phenomenal memory. Furthermore, he applied himself to his work with long hours and intense concentration. He knew far more about the country than anyone else. Trujillo was a credulous health cultist, fond of experimenting with new foods and rejuvenating drugs, and was a respected womanizer. As much wealth as he amassed, however, he was not overly self-indulgent or fond of luxury. A doer, a builder, a dynamo of a man, he had a compulsion to make things work the way he thought they should. The men about him, even the nominal presidents, might be the most abject of sycophants but they had to be efficient. Trujillo was merciless with the inept or the incompetent. The end to which his undoubted abilities were directed was not the justification of any political philosophy. It was, rather, the transformation of the pathetic little tropical republic into a modern business, perhaps to make it worthy of its ruler and owner.

A ruinous hurricane that struck Santo Domingo in September 1930 enabled Trujillo to set the pattern for his regime. His humanitarian labors created a favorable image at home and abroad, and his superb administrative gifts were employed to relieve the injured and desolate and to reconstruct the city. During the crisis he also acquired emergency powers which he never relinquished, and ridded himself of inconvenient persons. Stunning performance as a ruler, glorification of his deeds, and skill in removing opposition continued to characterize his regime. Trujillo had no inclination to share the burdens of power. His congresses were abject packs of nonentities, named in farcical elections and subject to instant removal at his whim. Debates dealt with trivial matters. The judiciary was a mere extension of the dictator, with judges being named and ousted according to a logic understood only by Trujillo. Local units of government were also subordinated to him. So were private or unofficial organizations, such as the confederation of labor unions, which was a mere showcase. Even the Church exercised its functions within the Trujillo consensus. A concordat signed in Rome by Trujillo and Pius XII in 1954 brought little advantage to the Church save freedom from overt persecution, and it was the occasion for legalizing one of Trujillo's divorces.

The army was obviously the most important element in the dictator's power structure. Officers were promoted and cashiered as casually as civilian officials. As long as they stood well with Trujillo they enjoyed opportunities for enrichment. So skilled was he in handling men that they never united against him. If they had, he was sure of the loyalty of the enlisted men, who had the best the little country could provide and who were, besides, indoctrinated in the cult of the Benefactor. And Trujillo distributed ammunition so parsimoniously that a revolt might be cut short at the outset. In addition to an obedient army, the tyrant enjoyed the services of as efficient a police force as the Caribbean knew, one that repeatedly bested the Communists and rival dictators in secret operations. Supported by terroristic gangs known as "The Forty-Two" and later as "The Veterans," it smelled plots before they materialized and frustrated popular manifestations and individual conspiracies. Many dubious accidents and suicides removed Trujillo's enemies at home and abroad. Dominican exiles were well aware of the omniscience of the police, which functioned effectively outside the republic and was seldom exposed.

Popularity was another source of Trujillo's strength. Until his last years it was generally believed that he was truly a benefactor. He invited poor families to name him the godfather of their children, an honor that brought them a bonus and that tens of thousands solicited. The condition of the working classes was greatly improved, partly because of the material progress but also because of favors. Welfare agencies were numerous and generous. Though the right to strike was not conceded, laborers had pensions, minimum wages, low-cost housing, and limited working hours. The humble knew that Trujillo had once been one of them, and they could vicariously identify themselves with his advancement. The middle classes grew considerably under the order and the good business conditions Trujillo had brought about. And the rich, a category whose number expanded from only a few families to many dozens, had wealth precisely because they cooperated with the dictator.

During the "Era of Trujillo" the Dominican Republic made great strides materially. The somnolent countryside gradually awoke as new agricultural methods, machinery, plants, and seeds were introduced. While most peasants still ate corn and cassava and lived in thatched huts, conditions were better than they had been and hopes were aroused. Small farms, to be sure, tended to be absorbed in larger concentrations, many of which were owned by the Trujillo clan and became models of modernity. The livestock industry likewise underwent a transformation as scientific breeding and better animal husbandry were popularized. Mining revived, with iron ore and bauxite proving profitable. New industries came into the island, mostly sugar-refining, food-processing, and the manufacture of cement and consumer articles. Commerce expanded steadily, multiplying almost twentyfold during the Trujillo years. More than half the exports were sugar products, with Great Britain the leading buyer; other exports were cacao, coffee, and tobacco, which went mainly to the United States, the source of most of the republic's imports.

Public works filled the land with the best roads in the Caribbean, as well as airports and wharves. Ciudad Trujillo was the cleanest city in the West Indies. Other Dominican towns had fine public buildings, though the taste of Trujillo-period architecture was vulgar, and wide streets fronting parks and a few modern homes and business buildings. Sanitary conditions were excellent for the tropics, enabling the population to increase 250 per cent during the Trujillo years. Public education received much favor, with the number of schools growing from 900 to 3,000 and the student population reaching almost a half-million. Illiteracy did not drop as much as Trujillo claimed, for the population growth taxed the school system; probably it did not fall below 60 per cent. And students spent as much time hearing of Trujillo's glory as they did learning to read and write. Even the ancient university, which received a handsome new suburban campus, asserted itself only to register awe and gratitude for the Benefactor.

Dominican culture has always been thin, but a few civilized individuals have generally been able to keep the small educated group abreast of currents abroad. Several Romantic poets appeared in the late nineteenth century. Early in the twentieth, Pedro and Max Henríquez Ureña introduced Modernism, a school that later attracted other Dominican poets. Fabio Fiallo, the poet who was imprisoned during the American occupation, was fairly famous in Latin America even before this incident. During the Trujillo dictatorship literature was largely reduced to glorifying the tyrant. Yet a circle of poets managed to commune with one another and to maintain democratic values as well as the conviction that their country might some day enjoy them. The most renowned writer of the period was a staunch enemy of Trujillo, the exiled Juan Bosch, whose short stories and novel established him as a worthy writer and brought him a fame that was helpful when he ran for president after Trujillo's death.

Peace and solid growth gave the regime a good reputation. It was with favor that the outside world noted how Trujillo negotiated the end of American fiscal controls in 1941, paid off all foreign debts with a check for $10 million in 1947, liquidated the internal debt in 1953, and kept the Dominican *peso* sound in an inflation-prone international economy. His offer to provide homes for 100,000 Jewish refugees in 1938 and for Hungarian victims in 1956 brought good publicity, though very few came. The loyal if ineffective participation of the republic in World War II was also an agreeable gesture. Trujillo was fashionably mellow toward Communism during the war years and until 1947, when he became a stalwart opponent. His friendship with Franco Spain and the concordat of 1954 reassured many conservatives. His worst crime was almost obscured by the greater enormities of the Axis at the time: in October 1937, two years after Haiti and the Dominican Republic had finally settled their historic boundary dispute, Trujillo set his soldiers on Haitian squatters on his side of the line and had perhaps 10,000 massacred. Compensation of $750,000 for these deaths, and friendly visits to Port-au-Prince afterward by Trujillo, did something to reduce the effect of the atrocity. And, as always, foreign journalists were receptive to subsidies in exchange for publicizing the Benefactor's other deeds.

Not until the late 1950s did American official and public opinion become seriously critical of Trujillo. By then there was an accumulation of plausible stories by Dominican refugees of oppression, evidence of meddling in the gangster politics of other Caribbean nations, and indications that the Trujillo family had become immensely wealthy. The decisive event in awakening American hostility was the disappearance of Jesús de Galíndez. An exiled Spanish republican, Galíndez had spent some years in Santo Domingo. Later he went to the United States, where he compiled a doctoral dissertation which exposed the Trujillo regime in a rather subdued fashion. One night in March 1956 he vanished in the New York subways. Later, an airplane pilot declared that he had flown Galíndez, kidnaped and drugged, to the Dominican Republic, whereupon the pilot was killed. Trujillo's implication was never proved; there was reason to suspect it and reason to doubt it. Yet the affair released a flood of other stories damaging to the dictatorship. In addition, the antics of Trujillo's son and namesake, "Ramfis," who achieved the distinction of being denied graduation from the U.S. Command and General Staff School, aroused more disapproval, as did the dictator's petulant reaction to American criticism. And then President Betancourt of Venezuela was injured and nearly killed by weapons from the Dominican Republic, surely at Trujillo's command.

Another factor in Trujillo's rapid fall in American esteem was the rise of Fidel Castro in Cuba. Many Americans objected to tolerating Trujillo while opposing Castro. Under United States prompting, the Organization of American States condemned both regimes in 1960 and, because of the attempt on Betancourt's life, broke relations with the Dominican Republic. Trujillo repudiated American economic assistance and made friendly overtures to the Communist bloc. Commerce fell off sharply and tourism all but ceased. Early in 1961 the Catholic clergy stunned the regime by denouncing it in Dominican churches. Still the aging despot presented an appearance of serene confidence. Mass demonstrations in his behalf seemed to indicate the abiding support of his people. And then, on the night of May 30,

1961, Trujillo was ambushed as he was being driven in an automobile on the outskirts of the capital to the home of his mistress. He emerged firing a pistol but was shot dead.

For some days the Dominicans seemed stupefied, even orphaned, by the loss of the Benefactor. His funeral was the occasion for an impressive popular demonstration of grief. Ramfis flew home from Europe to take charge of the armed forces and to punish his father's killers, some of whom were army and police officers. The president, Joaquín Balaguer, a literary figure who had long prostituted his talents in behalf of Trujillo, led the panegyrists in mourning his death. Gradually, he loosened the system of terror and began to voice criticisms of his late master, enough to assure an American mission that the dictatorship would not be perpetuated. In November the Trujillo family apparently decided to restore themselves to full power. The timely appearance of a United States task force gave Balaguer the courage to defeat and exile the Trujillos. Although their fortune of hundreds of millions in the Dominican Republic was to be confiscated, they apparently had great resources banked abroad.

In January 1962 Balaguer was ousted in a confused coup and Vice-President Rafael Bonnelly assumed the presidency. American recognition and aid, as well as the lifting of the OAS ban, invigorated the regime, and economic life began to revive. So did political life, so long smothered by the terrorism of Trujillo. Agitation for "de-Trujilloization," liberty, division of property, and better housing stirred the masses as the election of December 1962 loomed. In that test, the first free one since 1924, victory went to the scholarly Juan Bosch, who had been exiled since 1940 and who represented the liberal and leftist elements. Perhaps Bosch aroused too many hopes among the masses for speedy reform and regeneration, and too much apprehension among clerical and business circles. His few months of power were characterized by runaway leftist agitation, Communist boldness, and weak or inept administration. In September 1963 he was abruptly deposed and exiled by a military group, much to the displeasure of the United States. The new junta promised to hold free elections in 1965. The interruption of its plans occasioned by the rebellion of April and May and the startling American intervention with thousands of armed men dramatized the irregular nature of the little nation's political development, which had always been subject to sudden and disagreeable change. There was little to inspire optimism concerning the future of democratic institutions in the Dominican Republic. Though its economic base was sufficient to provide a livelihood for a rapidly growing population for some years, it was problematical whether the masses would be satisfied.

Cuba

Alone of the Caribbean island nations, Cuba has a very respectable body of historical literature. Several Spanish and creole works of the late colonial period are classics. Historians of Cuba, Spain, and the United States have written copiously about many aspects of the independence efforts of the nineteenth century and the war of 1898. Although they often disagree, their coverage of the period is complete enough to enable objective students to find their bearings. After Cuba became independent, her historians tended to write in a positivistic vein, glorifying the emancipation of their country and its apparent progress. Forming the Academy of History in 1910, they strove for integrity and accuracy, collected and published documents, and usually displayed an amiable attitude toward the United States. Very few American historians paid attention to the island's history after 1902 except for its relations with the United States.

As the twentieth century wore on, the neglect of foreign historians regarding Cuba became more pronounced, so that in most countries the crisis resulting from Fidel Castro's advent caught academic and intellectual circles lacking in knowledge of the island. This was scarcely the fault of Cuban writers, however, for they had been very active. A monumental ten-volume national history, published in 1952, did credit to the scholarship of Cuban historians, and many worthy monographs had also appeared.

Another trend, almost unnoticed outside Cuba but greatly influential on the youth of that country, was the populariation of a new interpretation. This intensified the anti-Spanish tradition that had long been familiar, but it further depicted the United States as a villain from about 1800 onward. A *Sociedad Cubana de Estudios Históricos e Internacionales* founded in 1940 attracted leftist historians and gave direction to their anti-Americanism. A series of congresses issued pronouncements that purported to settle questions long debated by scholars. Usually they attributed evil motives and harmful actions to the United States. By 1965, nearly all the traditionalist historians of Cuba were silent or in exile, and a number of the *Sociedad Cubana* revisionists had found Castroism too extreme an embodiment of attitudes they had fostered. Foreign historians were belatedly studying Cuba in the hope of understanding the forces behind its recent course.

Excellent summaries of Cuban historiography are found in Robert Freeman Smith, "Twentieth-Century Cuban Historiography," *Hispanic American Historical Review*, February 1964, pp. 44-73; Duvon C. Corbitt, "Cuban Revisionist Interpretations of Cuba's Struggle for Independence," *ibid.*, August 1963, pp 395-404; and, in a more extensive study, José Manuel Pirez Cabrera, *Historiografía de Cuba* (Mexico, 1962).

GENERAL: *Historia de la nación cubana* (10 vols., Havana, 1952), edited by several of Cuba's most respected historians with contributions by many writers, including a few of the revisionist school, is necessarily uneven in quality but is an admirable and complete treatment. Well-known textbooks are Ramiro Guerra y Sánchez, *Manual de historia de Cuba* (Havana, 1938); Fernando Portuondo del Prado, *Historia de Cuba* (5th ed., Havana, 1953); Emeterio S. Santovenia, *Historia de Cuba* (2 vols., Havana, 1939-43); and Emilio Roig de Leuchsenring (ed.), *Curso de introducción a la historia de Cuba* (Havana, 1938). A recent treatment, mainly political in emphasis is Carlos Márquez Sterling, *Historia de Cuba desde Colón hasta Castro* (New York, 1963). Herminio Portell Vilá, *Historia de Cuba en sus relaciones con los Estados Unidos y España* (4 vols., Havana, 1938-41) is a detailed study presenting the revisionist interpretation with anti-American bias. H. E. Friedlaender, *Historia económica de Cuba* (Havana, 1944) is rich and sound. Fernando Ortiz, *Cuban counterpoint: tobacco and sugar* (New York, 1947), is a famous work by a respected Cuban scholar. Philip S. Foner, *A history of Cuba and its relations with the United States* (2 vols., New York, 1962-63) carries the story to 1895 with projected volumes yet to come: an earnest effort to cover the subject in detail; Marxist, pro-Cuban, and rhetorical. Willis Fletcher Johnson, *The history of Cuba* (5 vols., New York, 1920) is old-fashioned and unprofessional, but still useful. Robert F. Smith (ed.), *What happened in Cuba? A documentary history* (New York, 1963) contains basic documents covering U.S.-Cuban relations from 1783 to 1962 with excellent comments.

PRIMITIVE: José Álvares Conde, *Arqueología Indocubana* (Havana, 1956); Mark Raymond Harrington, *Cuba before Columbus* (2 vols., New York, 1921); Fernando Ortiz, *Cuba primitiva* (Havana, 1922) and *Historia de la arqueología cubana* (Havana, 1936).

COLONIAL: Irene A. Wright, *The early history of Cuba, 1492-1586* (New York, 1916) is excellent. Pedro J. Guiteras, *Historia de la isla de Cuba*

(2 vols., New York, 1865-66) shows the creole mentality; Alexander von Humboldt, *The island of Cuba* (Tr. J. S. Thrasher, New York, 1856) gives a good picture of the island at the beginning of the 19th century; Jacobo de la Pesuela, *Historia de la isla de Cuba* (4 vols., Madrid, 1868-78) is a well-known account, rather pro-Spanish; José Antonio Saco, *Historia de la esclavitud* (6 vols., Barcelona, 1875-79) is also a general history, pro-creole.

On mid-century American involvement: Robert G. Caldwell, *The López expeditions to Cuba, 1848-1851* (Princeton, 1915); Herminio Portell Vilá, *Narciso López y su época* (3 vols., Havana, 1930-58); Basil Rauch, *American interest in Cuba: 1848-1855* (New York, 1948); and Emilio Roig de Leuchsenring, *Cuba y los Estados Unidos, 1805-1898* (Havana, 1949). Portell Vilá and Roig offer distorted interpretations of U.S. policies in many instances.

On the revolutionary movements: Vidal Morales y Morales, *Iniciadores y primeros martires de la revolución Cubana* (3 vols., Havana, 1931); Francisco Ponte Domínguez, *Historia de la guerra de los diez años* (2 vols., Havana, 1944-58); Ramiro Guerra, *Guerra de los Diez Años, 1868-1878* (2 vols., Havana, 1950); *Papeles de Maceo* (2 vols., Havana, 1948); *Papeles de Martí* (3 vols., Havana, 1933-35); Richard Butler Gray, *José Martí, Cuban patriot* (Gainesville, 1962), a superior analysis; *Epistolario de José Martí* (arranged by Félix Lizaso, Havana, 1930), with a useful chronology and other biographical details; Jorge Mañach, *Martí, el apóstol* (Havana, 1933), in the cult; R. H. Kimball, *Cuba, and the Cubans* (New York, 1880); and Murat Halstead, *The story of Cuba* (Chicago, 1896), a rambling but helpful work.

Three Spanish captain-generals of the late colonial period whose reports are significant are Miguel Tacón y Rosique, *Relación del gobierno . . .* (Mexico, 1838); José de la Concha, *Memorias. . . .* (Madrid, 1853); and Camilo de Polavieja, *Mi política en Cuba* (Madrid, 1898). Recommended accounts of Cuban history in the 19th century by Spaniards are Antonio Ballesteros Beretta, *Historia de España y su influencia en la historia universal,* Vol. XI (2nd ed., Barcelona, 1956); Antonio Pirala y Criado, *Anales de la guerra de Cuba* (3 vols., Madrid 1895-98); and Fernando Soldevila, *Historia de España,* Vol. VIII (Barcelona, 1959).

FROM COLONY TO PROTECTORATE: Valeriano Weyler, *Mi mando en Cuba* (5 vols., Madrid, 1910), an apologia by one of the most hated Spaniards; *The American-Spanish War* (Norwich, 1899), with articles by the major Cuban and American leaders in the conflict; Frank Freidel, *The splendid little war* (Boston, 1958), mainly a collection of sources, well-arranged; Alfred T. Mahan, *Lessons of the war with Spain* (Boston, 1899), a famous and influential work; Major General Joseph Wheeler, *The Santiago campaign* (Boston, 1898); Cosme de la Torriente, *Fin de la dominación española en Cuba* (Havana, 1948); Emilio Roig de Leuchsenring,

La guerra libertadora cubana de los trienta años 1868-1898 (Havana, 1952), a strident assertion that Cubans won their own independence and that the United States always opposed it; David F. Healy, *The United States in Cuba, 1898-1902* (Madison, 1963), a superior analysis and interpretation; *Final Report of Major General John R. Brooke* (Havana, 1899); Leonard Wood, *Annual Reports* (33 vols., Washington, 1900-1902).

THE REPUBLIC: Charles E. Chapman, A *history of the Cuban republic* (New York,1927) offers a detailed political history to Machado. Anecdotal, opinionated, patronizing toward Cuba, but indispensable. Russell H. Fitzgibbon, *Cuba and the United States, 1900-1935* (Menasha, 1935) is sound and solid but partially out of date. David A. Lockmiller, *Magoon in Cuba* (Chapel Hill, 1938), rehabilitates this maligned figure. Irene A. Wright, *Cuba* (New York, 1910), describes Cuba in the early days of the republic. Lowry Nelson, *Rural Cuba* (Minneapolis, 1950), gives an excellent picture from the sociologist's point of view. Robert F. Smith, *The United States and Cuba* (New Haven, 1960), a useful and detailed study of business and diplomacy from 1917 to 1960, critical of the Americans. Leland H. Jenks, *Our Cuban colony, a study in sugar* (New York, 1928) is good on the sugar industry but sensational about American pressures. Foreign Policy Association, *Problems of the new Cuba* (New York, 1935) provides an excellent description of Cuba's ills in the early Batista period. Harry F. Guggenheim, *The United States and Cuba* (New York, 1934) deals with the Machado period. R. Hart Phillips, *Cuban sideshow* (Havana, 1935) is useful on the fall of Machado and the revolution. Her *Cuba, island of paradox* (New York, 1959) carries the account to the advent of Castro. International Bank for Reconstruction and Development, *Report on Cuba* (Baltimore, 1951) is a well-known and highly reputable study of the island in 1950. Also of great value are the successive volumes edited by A. C. Wilgus on the Caribbean, published annually by the University of Florida Press since 1951.

Among Cuban writers José Manuel Carbonell, *Cuba independiente*, Vol. XII of Ricardo Levene (ed.) *Historia de América* (Buenos Aires, 1949) is good on the political history of the occupation and early years of the republic. Mario Riera Hernández, *Cuba política, 1899-1950* (Havana, 1959) contains election statistics and campaign data. Enrique José Varona y Pera, *De la colonia a la república* (Havana, 1919); León Primelles, *Crónica cubana, 1915-1918* (Havana, 1955) and *Crónica cubana, 1919-1922* (Havana, 1957); and Ramiro Guerra y Sánchez, *Sugar and society in the Caribbean, An economic history of Cuban agriculture* (New Haven, 1964) are invaluable. Edmund A. Chester, A *sergeant named Batista* (New York, 1954) is a romanticized account of Batista's career to the early part of his second dictatorship. Emilio Roig de Leuchsenring, *Males y vicios de Cuba republicana* (Havana, 1959) elaborates the writer's familiar theme concerning the harmful influence of the United States. *Revaloración de la historia de Cuba por los congresos nacionales de historia* (Havana, 1959) summarizes pronouncements by leftist Cuban historians in recent years. *Anuario azucarero de Cuba,* an annual publication since 1937 that reveals much about Cuba's sugar industry. *Anuario estadístico de Cuba* has useful annual statistics about the island.

THE CASTRO PERIOD: Fulgencio Batista Zaldívar, *Cuba betrayed* (New York, 1962), a disorganized apologia by the ruler Castro overthrew; Ray Brennan, *Castro, Cuba, and justice* (Garden City, 1959), a semi-fictional romanticization of Castro, scornfully denying his faults; David D. Burks, *Cuba under Castro* (New York, 1965), a short pamphlet but incisive and authoritative; Teresa Casuso, *Cuba and Castro* (New York, 1961), interesting on the bizarre life of a revolutionary who worked with Castro and later defected. Theodore Draper, *Castro's revolution: Myths and realities* (New York, 1962) is probably the most perceptive book on the subject, unfriendly to Castro but corrective of extreme criticisms of him. Foreign Policy Association, *The Cuban crisis, a documentary record* (New York, 1963) contains major papers on the confrontation of 1962. Haynes Johnson and others, *The Bay of Pigs, the leaders' story of Brigade 2506* (New York, 1964) is a moving account by the participants in the ill-fated landing. Herbert L. Matthews, *The Cuban story* (New York, 1961) is a famous and influential book by a well-known journalist who became a friend of Castro before his rise to power and remained very favorably disposed toward him. C. Wright Mills, *Listen, Yankee* (New York, 1960) seems to be the author's recollections of Castro's conversations with him, presented as the composite voice of Cuban critics of the United States. Irving Peter Pflaum, *Tragic island: How Communism came to Cuba* (Englewood Cliffs, 1961), is a thoughtful and balanced account of the Batista and early Castro period. R. Hart Phillips, *The Cuban dilemma* (New York, 1962) is a highly critical but sometimes naïve chronicle of Castro's first two years in power. Nicolás Rivero, *Castro's Cuba* (Washington, 1962) is a bitter account by a defector. Dudley Seers (ed.) *Cuba, The economic and social revolution* (Chapel Hill, 1964), a study by four Chilean and British writers with useful statistics, if they are accurate, and a somewhat sunny appraisal of Castro's achievements. Earl E. T. Smith. *The fourth floor* (New York, 1962), a pungent account by the U.S. ambassador to Cuba from 1957 to 1959 who early suspected Castro of Communism and alleges that second-level officials in Washington favored the Cuban revolutionary. Edwin C. Stein, *Cuba, Castro, and Communism* (New York, 1962) gives a harsh view of Castro. Tad Szulc and Karl Meyer, *The Cuban invasion: the chronicle of a disaster* (New York, 1962) is a well-informed study of the Bay of Pigs fiasco. Nathaniel Weyl, *Red star over Cuba* (New York, 1961) presents an unrestrained indictment of those who did not detect Castro's Communist ties from the first. William A. Williams, *The United States, Cuba, and Castro* (New York, 1962) shows the early enthusiasm for the Cuban revolution that was was typical of much of the academic community. Maurice Zeitlin and Robert Scheer, *Cuba: tragedy in our hemisphere* (New York, 1963) is very critical of American policy and optimistic about Castro. Ronald Hilton (ed.) *The Hispanic American Report*, a monthly summary of events during the year 1948-64 has immense value in studying the unfolding history of Cuba, Haiti, the Dominican Republic, and other Latin American countries.

CULTURE: Enrique Anderson-Imbert, *Spanish-American literature: A history* (Detroit, 1963); Adolfo Dollero, *Cultura cubana* (Havana, 1916); Wyatt MacGaffey and Clifford Barnett, *Cuba: Its people, its society, its culture* (New Haven, 1962), a well-written and thoughtful treatment; Fernando Ortiz, *Los bailes y el teatro de los negros en el folklore de Cuba* (Havana, 1951); Juan J. Remos, *Historia de la literatura cubana* (3 vols., Havana, 1945); Medardo Vitier, *Las ideas en Cuba* (2 vols., Havana, 1938); Max Henríquez Ureña, *Panorama histórico de la literatura cubana, 1492-1952* (New York, 1963), a reliable and thorough account of the colonial period, to be followed by a second volume on the republican.

Haiti

Emily Greene Balch (ed.) *Occupied Haiti* (New York, 1927), a work of much value by several contributors, suspicious and critical of the U.S. Government. Dantès Bellegarde, *La nation haïtienne* (Paris, 1938 and other editions), an adequate textbook. Donald B. Cooper, "The withdrawal of the United States from Haiti, 1928-1934," *Journal of Inter-American studies* (January 1963) is an incisive account. Louis E. Élie, *Histoire d'Haiti* (2 vols., Port-au-Prince, 1944-45), an elementary, general account, stressing the colonial period. Earl Leslie Gribbs and Clifford H. Prator (ed.) *Henry Christophe: Thomas Clarkson, a correspondence* (Los Angeles, 1952) is revealing about Christophe and his times. Melville J. Herskovits, *Life in a Haitian valley* (New York, 1937), mainly on voodoo, which is treated respectfully. S. L. R. James, *The Black Jacobins: Toussaint l'Ouverture and the San Domingo revolution* (2nd ed., New York, 1963), a fine study of Haiti and its chief hero. James G. Leyburn, *The Haitian people* (New Haven, 1941), a sound work on social conditions, by no means out-of-date. James H. McCrocklin, *Garde d'Haiti 1915-1934* (Annapolis, 1955), a thoughtful appraisal of the American-sponsored Haitian armed force and the occupation. Arthur C. Millspaugh, *Haiti under American control* (Boston, 1931), a careful, balanced treatment of the occupation. Medéric-Louis-Élie Moreau de Saint Méry, *Description topographique, physique, civile, politique, et historique de la Partie française de l'isle Saint-Domingue* (3 vols., new edition, Paris,

1958), a classic study of colonial Haiti on the eve of the French Revolution. David Placide, *L'heritage colonial en Haiti* (Madrid, 1959) is a fine study of social conditions. Sir Spenser St. John, *Hayti or the Black Republic* (London, 1884) has some value. Jean Price-Mars, *La république d'Haiti et la république dominicaine* (2 vols., Port-au-Prince, 1953) relates the conflicts of the two nations from the Haitian point of view. Selden Rodman, *Haiti: the black republic* (New York, 1954) is useful and readable but rather light. Francis Alexander Stanislaus, Baron de Wimpffen, *A voyage to Saint Domingo in the years 1788, 1789, and 1790*, translated by J. Wright (London, 1817): a good first-hand description of the colony in the first years of the Revolution. T. Lothrop Stoddard, *The French Revolution in San Domingo* (Boston, 1914), an indispensable account, detailed and solid, but marred by the author's thesis of Negro inferiority.

The Dominican Republic

Joaquín Balaguer, *Dominican reality: biographical sketch of a country and a regime* (Mexico, 1949) has some worthwhile details but is essentially a worshipful study of Trujillo. Juan Bosch, *Crisis de la democracia de la América en la República Dominicana* (Mexico, 1964) contains the reflections of the president elected in 1962 and deposed a few months later. Arthur J. Burks, *Land of checkerboard families* (New York, 1932), an anecdotal account by a U.S. Marine officer of the occupation. Arturo Espaillat, *Trujillo: the last Caesar* (Chicago, 1963), is a sensational account by a onetime Trujillo intelligence officer. Jesús de Galíndez Suárez, *La era de Trujillo: un estudio casuístico de dictadura hispano-americana* (Buenos Aires, 1956): this doctoral dissertation, an exposé of Trujillo not so damning as the dictator probably thought, may have led to its author's murder. Marvin Goldwart, "The constabulary in the Dominican Republic and Nicaragua," in *Latin American monographs*, No. 17 (Gainesville, 1962), an excellent study. Albert C. Hicks, *Blood in the streets* (New York, 1946), journalistic, anti-Trujillo. Melvin M. Knight, *The Americans in Santo Domingo* (New York, 1928) is a fine study of the occupation. Dana G. Munro, *Intervention and dollar diplomacy in the Caribbean, 1900-1921* (Princeton, 1964), a superior and authoritative work, rather favorable to U.S. policies, which also treats Cuba, Haiti, and other Caribbean countries. A. P. Newton *The European nations in the West Indies, 1493-1688* (London, 1933) contains a fine treatment of the early history of the Caribbean, particularly Hispaniola. J. H. Parry and P. M. Sherlock, *A short history of the West Indies* (London, 1956) is an excellent summary. Bernardo Pichardo, *Resúmen de la historia patria de la república dominicana* (3rd ed., Buenos Aires, 1947) is a textbook of some value. Germán E. Ornes, *Trujillo: Little Caesar of the Caribbean* (New York, 1958), a hostile account of the dictator. Selden Rodman, *Quisqueya, a history of the Dominican Republic* (Seattle, 1964), a readable survey. Otto Schoenrich, *Santo Domingo: a country with a future* (New York, 1918) has some interest. C. S. Tansill, *The United States and Santo Domingo, 1798-1873: a chapter in Caribbean diplomacy* (Baltimore, 1938) is careful and helpful. Stanley Walker, *Journey toward the sunlight* (New York, 1947), a shameful prostitution of the talents of a brilliant journalist in behalf of Trujillo. Sumner Welles, *Naboth's Vineyard: the Dominican Republic, 1844-1925* (2 vols., New York, 1928), a justly famous work by the eminent American diplomat.

Cuba

Haiti

The Dominican Republic

The Modern Nations in Historical Perspective Series